War for the Throne

Campaign Chronicles

Napoleon's Polish Gamble
Christopher Summerville

Armada 1588
John Barratt

Passchendaele
Martin Marix Evans

Attack on the Somme
Martin Pegler

Salerno
Angus Konstam

The Siege of Malta
David Williamson

The Battle of Borodino
Alexander Mikaberidze

Caesar's Gallic Triumph: Alesia 52BC
Peter Inker

Battle of the River Plate
Richard Woodman

The German Offensives of 1918
Ian Passingham

The Viking Wars of Alfred the Great
Paul Hill

Battle of North Cape
Angus Konstam

Dunkirk and the Fall of France
Geoffrey Stewart

Poland Betrayed
David Williamson

The Gas Attacks: Ypres 1915
John Lee

The Battle of the Berezina
Alexander Mikaberidze

Victory at Poitiers
Christian Teutsch

Campaign Chronicles

War for the Throne
The Battle of Shrewsbury 1403

John Barratt

Campaign Chronicles
Series Editor
Christopher Summerville

Pen & Sword
MILITARY

First published in Great Britain in 2010 by
Pen & Sword Military
an imprint of
Pen & Sword Books Ltd
47 Church Street
Barnsley
South Yorkshire S70 2AS

ISBN 978-1-84884-028-7

A CIP catalogue record for this book is available from the British Library.

Typeset in Sabon 11/13.5pt by
Concept, Huddersfield

Printed by the MPG Books Group
in the UK

Pen & Sword Books Ltd incorporates the imprints of Pen & Sword Aviation, Pen & Sword Maritime, Pen & Sword Military, Wharncliffe Local History, Pen & Sword Select, Pen & Sword Military Classics, Leo Cooper, Remember When, Seaforth Publishing and Frontline Publishing.

For a complete list of Pen & Sword titles please contact
PEN & SWORD BOOKS LIMITED
47 Church Street, Barnsley, South Yorkshire, S70 2AS, England
E-mail: enquiries@pen-and-sword.co.uk
Website: www.pen-and-sword.co.uk

Contents

Illustrations and Maps

Illustrations

Maps

War for the Throne

Illustrations and Maps

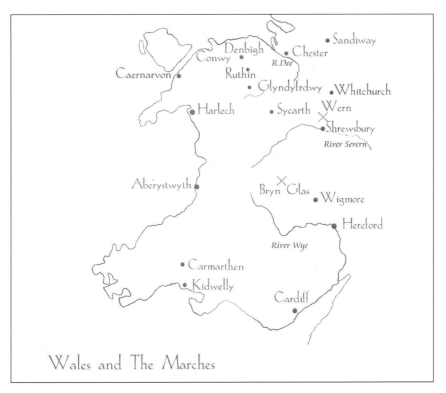

Sandiway

Denbigh • Chester
Conwy •
R.Dee

Caernarvon • Ruthin •

Glyndyfrdwy • Whitchurch

Harlech • Sycarth • Wern
✕
Shrewsbury

River Severn

Aberystwyth • ✕
Bryn Glas • Wigmore

Hereford •

River Wye

Carmarthen •
Kidwelly •

Cardiff •

Wales and The Marches

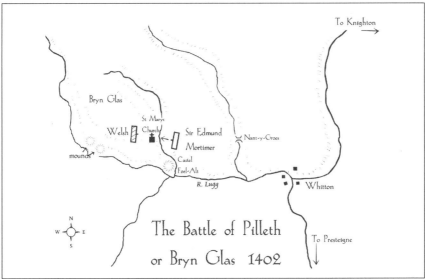

To Knighton →

Bryn Glas

St Marys
Welsh Church
Sir Edmund
Mortimer
Nant-y-Croes

mounds
Castel
Foel-Alt
R. Lugg
Whitton

N
W ✦ E
S

The Battle of Pilleth
or Bryn Glas 1402

To Presteigne ↓

ix

War for the Throne

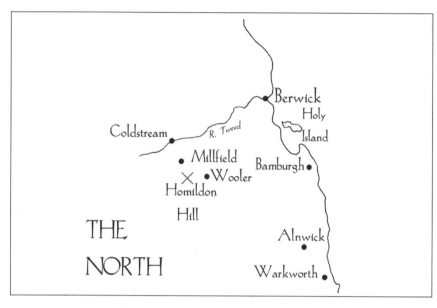

THE

NORTH

Coldstream
R. Tweed
Berwick
Holy
Island
Millfield
Bamburgh
Wooler
X
Homildon
Hill
Alnwick
Warkworth

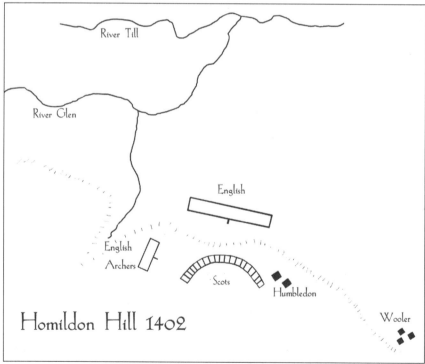

Homildon Hill 1402

River Till
River Glen
English
English
Archers
Scots
Humbledon
Wooler

Illustrations and Maps

Shrewsbury

The Campaign

6th July - 10th July

1403

1. 6 July. Glyn Dwr at Carmarthen Plant Owain (Owain s Children) raid across SW Wales
2. 9 July. King reaches Higham Ferrars (Beds.)
3. Hotspur rides south and reaches Chester 9 July
4. Earl of Northumberland reaches Warkworth
   c.10 July

Cocklaw

Hotspur

Warkworth
Alnwick

④

Earl

Neville Healaugh

York

③

Chester

P. Hen

Glyn Dwr Shrewsbury

①

Higham Ferrers

Northampton ②

Carmarthen

Eng. Garrisons

King

Bristol

London

War for the Throne

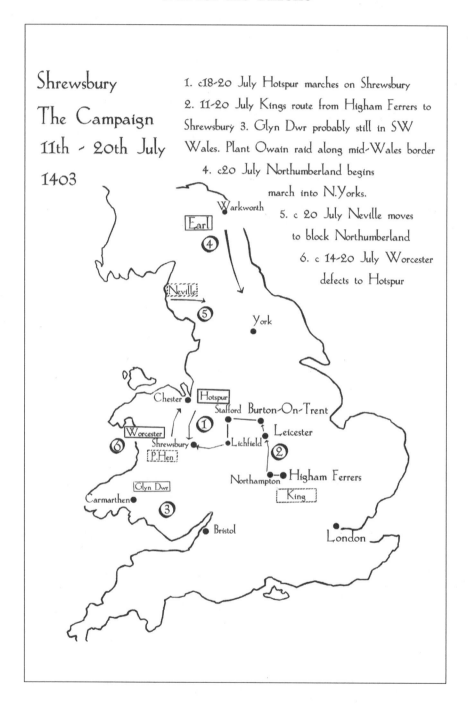

Shrewsbury

The Campaign

11th - 20th July

1403

1. c18-20 July Hotspur marches on Shrewsbury
2. 11-20 July Kings route from Higham Ferrers to Shrewsbury 3. Glyn Dwr probably still in SW Wales. Plant Owain raid along mid-Wales border
4. c20 July Northumberland begins march into N.Yorks.
5. c 20 July Neville moves to block Northumberland
6. c 14-20 July Worcester defects to Hotspur

Warkworth

Earl ④

Neville →
⑤

York

Chester • Hotspur
Stafford Burton-On-Trent
① •
Lichfield Leicester
Worcester
⑥ Shrewsbury • ② •
P.Hen
Northampton • Higham Ferrers
Glyn Dwr King
Carmarthen •
③
• Bristol
London

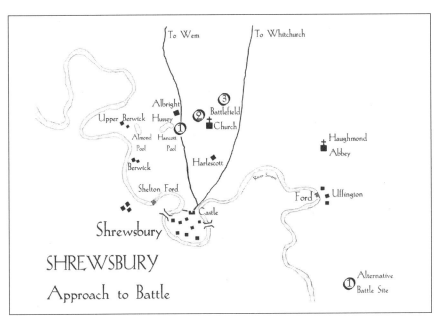

SHREWSBURY

Approach to Battle

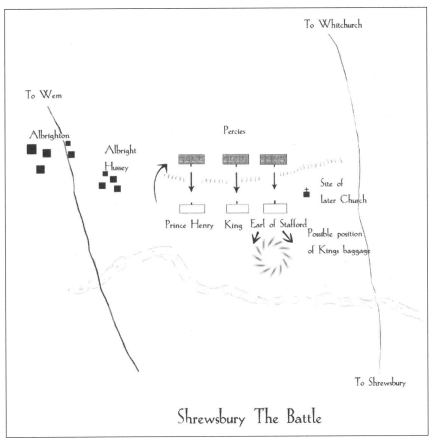

Shrewsbury The Battle

Chronology

1367 Birth of Henry Bolingbroke (King Henry IV).

1377 Accession of Richard II.

1387 Lords Appellant limit Richard's powers.

1388 Battle of Otterburn (5 August).

1398 Henry Bolingbroke exiled; death of John of Gaunt.

1399 Henry Bolingbroke returns; deposition of Richard II; Bolingbroke crowned as Henry IV.

1400
January: Pentecost Plot against Henry foiled.
February: Richard II probably murdered; unsuccessful campaign against Scots.
September: rebellion of Owain Glyn Dwr begins; first *chevauchée* by Henry IV.

1401
April: Welsh surprise Conwy Castle; Glyn Dwr rebellion spreads into Central Wales; Ricardian plotting in England continues.
October: Henry's second Welsh expedition.

1402
Further Ricardian conspiracies.
22 June: Battle of Bryn Glas – Welsh defeat and capture Sir Edmund Mortimer.
September: Henry IV's third Welsh expedition.

War for the Throne

14 September: Battle of Homildon Hill – Percys defeat the Scots.

October–December: king refuses to ransom Sir Edmund Mortimer; tensions rise with Hotspur over Scottish prisoners.

1403

March: king grants Percys any lands they conquer in Scotland; throughout the spring and early summer growing tensions between king and Percys over money.

May: Prince Henry destroys Glyn Dwr's homes at Sycarth and Glyndyfrdwy.

July: Glyn Dwr campaigns in South Wales.

10 July: Hotspur begins rebellion at Chester.

12 July: rumours of revolt reach the king at Nottingham.

17 July: Hotspur's forces rendezvous at Sandiway; king at Lichfield.

20 July: Hotspur arrives before Shrewsbury but refused entry; king arrives at Haughmond Abbey.

21 July: Battle of Shrewsbury.

23 July: Earl of Worcester and other rebel leaders executed.

August: Earl of Northumberland submits to king at York.

September: King Henry's fourth Welsh campaign.

1404

January: Northumberland pardoned by Parliament.

Spring: Glyn Dwr takes Harlech and Aberystwyth Castles and probably crowned as Prince of Wales.

Summer: Glyn Dwr holds Parliament at Machynlleth; in control of most of Wales.

1405

February: attempt to take Earl of March to Wales fails; Tripartate Indenture between Glyn Dwr, Mortimer and Northumberland.

11 April: Welsh defeated by Prince Henry at Grosmont.

May: Welsh defeat at Pwll Melyn; Rising in North Yorkshire headed by Richard Scrope, Archbishop of York, and the Earl Marshal, with Percy involvement.

6 June: Scrope and Earl Marshal captured and executed two days later; Northumberland and Lord Bardolph flee to Scotland.

Summer: Percy castles surrender.

Chronology

August: French forces land in Pembrokeshire to support Glyn Dwr; Franco-Welsh army advances to Woodbury Hill before returning to Wales; king's fifth Welsh expedition.

1406

Further reverses for Glyn Dwr; Anglesey and parts of South Wales submit to king.

1407

Further Welsh defeats; First Siege of Aberystwyth Castle.

1408

Northumberland and Bardolph rebel in the north; defeated and both killed at Bramham Moor 19 February; Second Siege of Aberystwyth, which falls c. September; Siege of Harlech begins.

1409

February: fall of Harlech; death of Sir Edmund Mortimer; Glyn Dwr reverts to guerrilla warfare.

1410

Last major Welsh raid on Shropshire defeated; death of Henry IV; Glyn Dwr rejects offer of pardon from Henry V; probable death of Glyn Dwr; son Maredudd continues to resist.

1421

8 April: Submission of Maredudd ab Owain marks effective end of organized Welsh rebellion.

Background

The great battles of the dynastic struggle, known as the 'Wars of the Roses', between the Houses of Lancaster and York in the second half of the fifteenth century are well known to most people with an interest in British history. But while Bosworth Field and Towton, Tewkesbury and Barnet, may be familiar, less well known is the desperate conflict of the early years of the same century, when the new Lancastrian dynasty, headed by King Henry IV – in the eyes of many of his reluctant subjects stained with the blood of the deposed and murdered Richard II – fought a merciless struggle for survival against a host of enemies at home and abroad. For almost a decade the issue remained in doubt. These years saw a war to the death between the new dynasty and its erstwhile supporters, the powerful Percy family (the 'Kings of the North'), a Scottish invasion, and the astonishing string of victories – almost realizing his dream of an independent Wales – won by that master of guerrilla warfare, Owain Glyn Dwr. The climax of the struggle, and the moment when King Henry came closest to death in battle, occurred on 21 July 1403, on Shakespeare's 'bloody field by Shrewsbury'. The battle (the first in which the famed English archers turned their missiles on each other) horrified contemporaries with its ferocity.

This book aims to bring the story of these dramatic years, and the colourful personalities – Kings Richard and Henry, the ruthless and devious Henry, Earl of Northumberland and his son, the impetuous Hotspur, the future King Henry V, and the charismatic and mysterious Glyn Dwr, before a wider audience. As ever, my thanks are due to

War for the Throne

Rupert Harding, Christopher Summerville and the rest of the team at Pen and Sword. And to Louisa Livingstone for her excellent maps, as well as the staff of the Sydney Jones Library, University of Liverpool, the British Library and Denbighshire County Libraries.

John Barratt

Henllan, May 2009.

Death of a King

The chain of events that would eventually climax in Shakespeare's 'bloody field by Shrewsbury' began almost thirty years earlier with the death, worn out by war and disease, of Edward the Black Prince, the able and popular son of King Edward III, likewise now approaching his end. As a result, on the king's death in 1377, the English throne passed to the Black Prince's 10-year-old son, Richard, and in practice, for some years to come, to three 'continual councils'. Considerable power also lay in the hands of Richard's uncle, John of Gaunt, Duke of Lancaster.

Richard's accession was greeted with considerable popular enthusiasm, and in 1381 his position was strengthened by the cool head he displayed during the crisis of the Peasants' Revolt. He promised pardon to the rebels but this pledge was promptly broken (it remains unclear whether Richard made his original promise in good faith). The episode was an early lesson in the cynical realities of medieval politics, which Richard fully absorbed.

As Richard grew towards manhood it was clear to the increasingly concerned members of his council, and the leading English nobility, that the king was both headstrong and determined to exert his own authority. He increasingly ignored the views of leading magnates, such as the Earl of Warwick, the Earl of Arundel and the Duke of Gloucester. Instead, Richard turned to his circle of favourites. These were mainly young and inexperienced men, chief among them Richard de Vere, Earl of Oxford, and Michael de la Pole, who Richard created Earl of Suffolk and made Chancellor of England. Rumours grew of a homosexual relationship between Richard and de Vere, adding to the growing concern and distrust felt by many towards the king.

Background

Shakespeare and History

William Shakespeare's *King Henry IV: Part One* was probably written in 1596–1597, as part of his cycle of plays charting the fifteenth-century struggle for the crown he commenced with his *King Richard II* in the previous year. Shakespeare took most of his historical information for the play from the extremely popular 'Chronicles' of Tudor historian Raphael Holinshead, and repeats his inaccuracies. He also takes a number of historical liberties for dramatic purposes. First and foremost he makes Hotspur a contemporary of Prince Hal, not of Henry IV, in order to provide a chivalric contrast to the dissolute young prince. The famous 'Sir John Falstaff' was originally named after the rebel and Lollard leader, Sir John Oldcastle, but rechristened following protests from the latter's descendants. In other respects Shakespeare follows the course of history reasonably accurately, and gives a particularly sympathetic portrait of Owain Glyn Dwr, possibly as a compliment to Queen Elizabeth with her partly Welsh ancestry in mind.

Richard's opponents among the nobility, among them John of Gaunt's son, Henry Bolingbroke, formed a group known as the Lords Appellant. Among their main grievances were Richard's plans to end the long-running war with France, where they still hoped for military success and financial reward.

In 1386 the Lords Appellant, through Parliament, called upon Richard to dismiss his unpopular councillors. Richard refused but was told that, as he was still technically a minor, a council of government would be appointed to rule in his name. The furious king reacted by arresting the leading Lord Appellant, the Earl of Arundel, and ordering de Vere to raise an army in the strongly Ricardian county palatine of Cheshire, and then to march on London. But in August 1387, de Vere was intercepted at Radcot Bridge near Oxford by the Lords Appellant, among them Henry Bolingbroke, and quickly routed. Richard himself was briefly imprisoned in the Tower of London, and, possibly under the threat of deposition, forced to accept the demands of the Lords Appellant.

War for the Throne

Richard's circle of advisers were removed from office, some being executed on charges of treason, and others exiled by what was known as the 'Merciless Parliament' of 1388. Richard was forced to accept new councillors and, for the moment, was stripped of most of his authority.

The events of 1387–1388 had shocked Richard, although he remained resolute that, sooner or later, revenge would be exacted upon those who had humiliated him. But for the present, he had to tread carefully, and, superficially, appeared to be reconciled with his principal opponents. However, many of the 'old' nobility continued to have a low opinion of a king whose interests lay in the world of the arts and culture rather than in war, which had been the main pursuit of his father and grandfather. He was compared ominously with his equally unpopular predecessor, King Edward II, who had been deposed and possibly murdered. Worse, Richard's few military ventures, such as his Scottish campaign of 1385, had proved humiliating failures, while in 1396 he made a 28-year truce with France, which was widely unpopular.

Meanwhile, Richard was becoming obsessed with a vision of the divine role of monarchy, which also led to him becoming increasingly impatient and intolerant of any attempt to restrict his authority. He revived and extended many aspects of kingship, becoming increasingly arrogant and distant towards his subjects, apart from the new group of favourites with whom he surrounded himself, and whose counsel could be relied upon to be what the king wanted to hear.

By the early 1390s Richard was emphasizing that, in his interpretation, his royal prerogative overrode the wishes and views of his subjects in an increasing number of areas, and reacted harshly to any attempts to challenge him. In 1392 he alienated the citizens of London by depriving them of many of their rights, after they refused to give him a loan. At the same time, his unpopularity also grew as a result of the increasing extravagance, and consequent cost, of the royal court. Richard reneged on promises that he had made to lower the burden of taxation imposed on his subjects. Instead, between 1390 and 1398, Parliament was forced to grant him four and a half subsidies.

By 1397, Richard's power seemed absolute, although his underlying insecurity and suspicion was emphasized by the recruitment of his

Background

notorious Cheshire Guard of archers, whose excesses, albeit at times exaggerated, served still further to increase Richard's unpopularity. Richard now moved against his old enemies, the Lords Appellant. On the pretext of a plot, which had probably not progressed much further than mutterings of discontent, the king had the principal Lords Appellant – Arundel, Warwick and Gloucester – arrested on charges of treason. After a show trial, Arundel was executed, and his brother, the archbishop of Canterbury, exiled. The Earl of Warwick, imprisoned in the English garrison of Calais, died in mysterious circumstances, almost certainly killed on Richard's orders, while the Duke of Gloucester, after abject pleas for mercy, was exiled for life. The confiscated estates of the Lords Appellant and their supporters were used to reward Richard's own adherents.

One complicating factor was that Richard was still childless. There were two possible successors to the throne. The strongest claim lay with the powerful Mortimer family, descended from King Edward III's brother, Lionel. Until 1398 the Mortimers were headed by Roger Mortimer, Earl of March, but his death left as heir his 7-year-old son, Edmund. Possibly because Edmund's youth prevented him from being a serious threat to his own position, Richard appeared to favour his eventual succession.

Two Lords Appellant remained. In 1387 both Henry Bolingbroke and Thomas Mowbray, Earl of Norfolk, had been junior members of the group. But this would not be enough to save them from Richard's vengeance. Furthermore, Bolingbroke, as son of Richard's uncle, John of Gaunt, had his own claim to the English throne; and as a man with a formidable military record abroad and considerable wealth, influence and popularity at home, was seen by Richard as a serious threat.

Neither Mowbray nor Henry can have had any illusions regarding the danger they were in. It could only be a matter of time before Richard moved against them. In the event, they obligingly toppled each other. According to the version of events that John of Gaunt related to the king, Mowbray approached Bolingbroke in December 1397, warning that Richard's plan was 'to do with us what he has done with the others. He wants to wipe clean any trace of our opposition'. On hearing what had happened, Mowbray presented the king with

The Cheshire Guard

With its long tradition of military service to the Plantagenet dynasty and its tradition of breeding hardened military men, Cheshire was a natural choice of recruiting ground when, in 1397, faced by growing domestic opposition, King Richard II decided to recruit a bodyguard loyal only to him. In July, Richard ordered the Sheriff of Chester to muster 2,000 archers for royal service, with the initial task of protecting the temporary hall erected at Westminster for the trial of the Lords Appellant. The force raised was said to include 'many malefactors out of the county of Cheshire, not gentlemen, but countrymen, cobblers, and other tradesmen'.

Richard now decided to raise a permanent bodyguard from Cheshire. Between September 1397 and 1398, 750 men were retained. They were formed into seven companies, or 'watches', each of around 100 men. All their commanders were minor Cheshire gentry, some professional soldiers, some of the men in each company being their own relatives or personal retainers.

The men of the Guard wore Richard's livery of either the White Hart or a crown. Their loyalty was ensured, not only by regular pay, but by the award of property forfeited by criminals or minor royal offices in Cheshire and elsewhere. The Guard was in constant attendance on the king – at night, one company, armed with large battleaxes – would stand guard over the royal quarters.

As with his other close retainers, Richard was reputedly on close personal terms with the archers of the Cheshire Guard. According to one hostile chronicler

> They were on such familiar terms with the lord king that they boldly addressed him in the mother tongue: 'Dycun, slep sicurly quile we wake, and dred nonst quile we live seftow, for zil thow haddest wedded Perkyn dauzer of Lye [Peter Lye was Richard's principal Cheshire recruiting agent] thow mun well halde a love day with any man in Chester in ffaith.' ['Dickon, sleep soundly while we wake, and dread nothing whilst we live, for as if you had married Perkyn, daughter of Lye, you could well have a love day with any man in [Cheshire] in faith.']

Background

Like similar units throughout history, the men of the Cheshire Guard acquired a notorious reputation. Among the crimes they were accused of were theft, robbery, rape and murder, for which Richard left them unpunished. There were certainly some instances of crimes committed by members of the Cheshire Guard, but claims that the king deliberately recruited criminals seem unfounded. The Guard was drawn from a wide spectrum of Cheshire society, ranging upwards from men renting their land and only owning a couple of cows, through to reasonably prosperous members of the yeoman class.

It should also be remembered that many of the Guard were professional soldiers, of a type used to enforcing their wishes by violence, but overall there is little evidence to suggest their behaviour was notably better or worse than that of other contemporaries of similar background.

his own version of the conversation, and apparently threw himself on Richard's mercy – never a bright option. On 19 March 1398, a Parliamentary commission decreed that the dispute should go before the court of chivalry: that is, that the issue be settled by single combat between the disputants.

The duel was to take place on 16 September, in Coventry. But as Mowbray and Henry prepared to face each other on the tournament ground, Richard intervened. Mowbray was to be banished from England for life, Henry for ten years.

Richard had disposed of two principal potential opponents. But his actions against Henry were widely perceived as a grave injustice and boosted Bolingbroke's already significant popularity among people of all social classes.

On 3 February 1399 Henry suffered a further blow when his father, John of Gaunt, died. Six weeks later, Richard announced that Henry was to be regarded as a traitor, all his possessions forfeited, and he himself banished for life.

Richard was so sure of his hold on England that he embarked on a full-scale military expedition to Ireland. He took with him as hostage

War for the Throne

Bolingbroke's 12-year-old son, Henry of Monmouth, and most of his own loyalists, leaving his uncle, the Duke of York, to maintain control in England.

It was at this point (if not earlier) that Henry decided to return to England, to regain what he saw as his own. Around 4 July 1399, he landed at Ravenspur on the River Humber in Yorkshire, with around 300 followers.

Although aware of the discontent felt in England towards Richard, Henry was nonetheless taking a desperate gamble. It is unclear what his exact intentions were at this point. But around 15 July, as growing numbers of supporters joined him, Henry could delay no longer in making his objectives clear.

The most powerful of those who had joined Bolingbroke were Henry, Earl of Northumberland, and his eldest son, Sir Henry Percy, better known as 'Hotspur'. Although the earl had experienced the customary military service associated with men of his rank, he was now over 50 years old, and concentrated on administering and extending the family estates. He seems to have been a canny if unscrupulous individual. Henry Percy's character was implied by his nickname of 'Hotspur' – supposedly given him by the Scots, with whom he was engaged in conflict for most of his life. A contemporary of Henry Bolingbroke, Hotspur was, in 1399, the military leader of the Percy dynasty. He had fought in France and elsewhere in Europe, although it was in the endemic raid and counter-raid of Scottish border warfare that he was best known. A brave and ferocious fighter, Hotspur seems to have had a tendency to impulsiveness, which in 1388, had led to his defeat and capture at Otterburn (*see text box*). His marriage to Elizabeth, sister of Roger Mortimer, linked the Percys to a family with claims to the English throne.

With huge estates in Yorkshire and Northumberland, the Percys were popularly known as the 'Kings of the North'. In fact, they were less secure than this title might suggest. Traditionally they held the office of Warden of the East March of the Scottish border, including the town of Berwick-upon-Tweed, and their own string of castles at Alnwick, Bamburgh, Warkworth and elsewhere. At times the crown also granted them the equally important post of Warden of the West March, with its headquarters at Carlisle.

The Battle of Otterburn 5 August 1388

In 1388 the Scots decided to take advantage of political dissent in England by launching a two-pronged raid across the border into the Northern English counties with the aim of inflicting maximum damage and forcing England formally to recognize Scotland as an independent sovereign state.

The main attack was launched on the West March, south beyond Carlisle, meeting with no serious resistance. The second thrust, on the East March, led by James, 2nd Earl of Douglas, was evidently intended rather more as a diversion. Douglas crossed the border sometime between 28 July and 1 August and, advancing rapidly, drove south, deep into County Durham, burning, killing, and driving off livestock.

The Scottish incursion caught the English off-balance. Although Hotspur was gathering a large force at Newcastle upon Tyne, he was supposed to await reinforcements under King Richard before taking the offensive. But events developed otherwise. Returning northwards, Douglas and his men appeared before the walls of Newcastle, halting to give time for their convoys of looted livestock to gain a head start on the road back to Scotland. There was some skirmishing with Hotspur. According to Froissart, this resulted in a personal encounter between Hotspur and Douglas, in which the Englishman was worsted, losing his lance pennon.

Whether or not this was so, when the Scots resumed their march north on 4 August, Hotspur was determined to pursue them and bring them to battle without waiting for further reinforcements. The Scots had halted at Otterburn, where the day was spent in ineffectual attempts to capture the small castle there. The Scots army probably totalled around 2,400 men, while Hotspur, who had apparently only brought mounted troops with him, most likely had very few more. The English force arrived at Otterburn around 8pm, with roughly an hour of daylight to bring the enemy to battle. The Scots were in two roughly fortified camps. One of them, on marshy ground, was occupied by servants and possibly some rank-and-file spearmen. Separate, on higher ground, was the camp of the nobles and men-at-arms.

War for the Throne

Hotspur split his force in two, sending a detachment under Sir Matthew Redman, to attack the servants' camp on the opposite side from his main force. But eager to gain a decision before nightfall, Hotspur waited neither for Redman to be in position or for stragglers who were still arriving. Though surprised, the Scots servants resisted for long enough for the men-at-arms in the higher camp hastily to arm themselves and join the fray.

The darkness evidently prevented the English from employing archery, and Douglas led a counter-attack against the English flank. The battle quickly became a confused and bloody mêlée, with the Scots gradually gaining the upper hand. Douglas was killed but reinforcements under the Earl of March arrived and made another attack that broke the English. Hotspur was taken prisoner.

Sir Matthew Redman's detachment was able to make a fighting withdrawal, though a total of 500 English dead were claimed by the Scots.

Hotspur was quickly ransomed, with assistance from the king, and Otterburn had no long-term significance, other than an indication of Hotspur's inclination to rashness, and the military ability of George Dunbar, Earl of March.

The problem for any monarch was that, if the Percys controlled the entire Scottish border and its resources in fighting men, they would be powerful enough to threaten the crown itself. Richard had never entirely trusted the Percys, whose evidently uncultivated northern ways and accents were regarded as alien in the sophisticated royal court, which heightened the unease of Northumberland and his son. Concerned about their near-monopoly of power in the north, Richard had given the Wardenship of the West March to Richard Neville, and although Sir Thomas Percy, brother of the Earl of Northumberland and a noted soldier and diplomat, was in the service of King Richard, the Percy family was never part of the royal inner circle, and there had recently been rumours that the king suspected them of treacherous intent.

The Percys seldom acted from motives other than self-interest, and their decision to join Henry Bolingbroke soon after his arrival in England was undoubtedly based on a realistic appraisal of his prospects of success. Percy military manpower also provided Henry

Background

with the bulk of his army, and left Northumberland and Hotspur in a powerful position to impose their views on Bolingbroke.

This was the background to the famous, and later much-disputed, oath that Bolingbroke swore in the house of the White Friars at Doncaster on 16 July. Its exact terms remain unclear. The Percys would later claim that Henry had sworn not to seize the throne, 'and if anyone could be found who was more worthy of the crown than he was, he would willingly stand down for him; the duchy of Lancaster was all that he wished for'. Indeed the pro-Percy chronicler, John Hardynge, went further and asserted that Henry intended to allow Richard to retain the throne, under the firm control of himself and the nobility and senior clergy.

All in all, it seems that whatever oath Henry actually swore was intended as a compromise, designed not to frighten off potential supporters by actually spelling out his intent to depose Richard, and probably in deference to the wishes of the Percys, leaving open the question – in the event that Richard was removed – of who should actually succeed him.

It was probably as he marched south – to be met with a groundswell of popular support and a growing flood of defections by Richard's former supporters – that Henry realized his position to be strong enough to gain the throne by popular acclamation.

Henry and his forces reached Leicester on 20 July. Edmund Duke of York, Richard's uncle, was at Berkeley Castle, near Bristol. He had failed to muster a significant army and his only hope of countering Henry's march south would have been if Richard and the army from Ireland had joined him. In any case, York had little enthusiasm for opposing Henry Bolingbroke, who was also his nephew. He made no attempt to oppose Henry's march south and on 27 July joined him. Bristol itself, where some of Richard's favourites had taken refuge, fell without a fight and Richard's captured supporters were arrested and executed.

Richard's kingdom was rapidly slipping from his grasp, and by the time he and his troops landed at Milford Haven in south-west Wales at the end of July, his cause already effectively lost. Apparently hoping to rally support in the Ricardian heartland of Cheshire, and fearful of betrayal (with good cause), the king abandoned his army and headed

War for the Throne

for North Wales with a handful of supporters. It was at best a forlorn hope, and with no sign of the hoped-for support, Richard took refuge in Edward I's great fortress of Conwy Castle.

Henry and his supporters were also heading north, in order to secure control of Cheshire. En route the Percys received what they probably saw as the first instalment of their expected reward, when the Earl of Northumberland, in an act implicit of Henry's intention to be king (at least in all but name) was granted the Wardenship of the West March of the Scottish border.

Chester surrendered to Henry without resistance. A desperate and despairing Richard sent the Dukes of Exeter and Surrey to Chester, offering to restore Henry to his lands and titles if he would submit and disband his army. It was a proposal that never had the slightest prospect of being accepted and the dukes were summarily imprisoned.

Richard was now without hope. He could, however, have stood siege in Conwy for some time, and Henry needed a quick conclusion before Richard's supporters elsewhere might rally. Around 15 August he sent the Earl of Northumberland and a body of troops to Conwy with instructions to lure Richard out of the castle and then detain him. Northumberland, with his proven qualities of deviousness and ruthlessness, was an excellent choice for the task. In tactics reminiscent of those employed in Scottish border warfare, Northumberland placed most of his men in ambush under the cover of high ground just east of the River Conwy, then gained an audience with Richard. Northumberland assured him that Henry wanted no more than his inheritance, proposing that Richard and Henry should ride together to London to hold a Parliament at which these proposals would be enacted, and apparently swore an oath to this effect on some holy relics.

Whether or not Richard was convinced, he had little option but to appear to agree, although one version of events has him telling the Earl of Salisbury that he would persuade Henry to march south via Wales, where Welsh supporters would ambush and capture him:

> I swear to you, that whatever assurances I may give him, he shall surely be put to a bitter death for this outrage and injury that he has done to us. Doubt it not, there shall be no Parliament held at Westminster on this matter.

Background

If indeed spoken they were words that clearly demonstrated that the conspirators would never be secure while Richard remained on the throne.

In the event, Richard rode east out of Conwy with Northumberland and was secured by Northumberland's men and taken to Flint Castle. Here, on 16 August, the trapped king saw the full strength of Henry's army taking up position around the castle. He was clearly doomed and, in despair, apparently refused all food. Henry entered the castle and allegedly assured Richard that he had come as a result of the discontent of the English people with Richard's rule: 'I will help you to govern them better than they have hitherto been governed.'

Richard once again had no choice but to agree, and was taken to Chester on the first stage of his journey to London. But there was soon a reminder that by no means all of Richard's supporters had accepted their master's fall. On the night of 21 August, one day after the party left Chester, a group of Richard's supporters – probably men of his Cheshire Guard – made an unsuccessful attempt to free him, and on the 23rd, at Lichfield, Richard made a thwarted effort to escape. For the remainder of the journey he was kept under close guard.

The pretence that Richard might remain king was already fading, and was weakened still further by the furious reception he met from the hostile London crowds as he was taken to confinement in the Tower. Henry, in contrast, received a rapturous welcome.

Even now, however, Henry's intentions regarding the crown were unclear. It was obvious that his actions up to this point had met with the active support and approval not only of his peers, but also of the majority of people of all classes. Of the other two possible replacements for Richard, Edmund Earl of March was too young, and Edmund, Duke of York, too old to be desirable choices. This left Henry himself, a popular and notable soldier and administrator, in the prime of life. By 10 September the decision had been taken to depose Richard. The delegation headed by the Earls of Northumberland and Westmoreland sent to persuade Richard to resign the throne initially met with a defiant response, but under continued pressure, he wavered and signed the document of abdication.

On 30 September, in Westminster Hall, after a long list of charges against Richard had been read out, Henry stepped forward to claim the throne amid great enthusiasm from those assembled and from the crowd outside. He was crowned king on 13 October in Westminster Abbey, the Earl of Northumberland, clearly supporting Henry's accession, carrying the Lancaster Sword at the head of the procession. But it was claimed by some that Hotspur – probably because of his Mortimer connection – absented himself from the ceremony.

There remained the question of what to do with Richard. His leading supporters were detained while their fate was considered. On 27 October the lords and prelates informed Parliament that the ex-king should be 'kept under safe and close guard, in some place where there was no coming and going of people; and that he should be guarded by reliable and competent men [. . .] in the most secret manner possible'.

Richard was eventually confined in the Lancastrian fortress of Pontefract Castle in Yorkshire. His leading supporters, while forfeiting any titles or lands gained since September 1397, were released. This would prove to be a grave error.

By the end of 1400 the leading 'Counter-Apellants', as they were known, joined by a squire named Richard Maudeleyn – who bore a close resemblance to Richard – were actively conspiring to assassinate King Henry and his four sons, who were celebrating Christmas at Windsor, and to secure London and other major towns, using Maudeleyn to impersonate Richard until the ex-king could be located and released. However, early in January, one of the conspirators, the former Duke of Aumale, betrayed the plot. Henry acted promptly, while, apart from a brief rising by Richard's supporters in Cheshire, the plotters failed to gain any real support. Some of their leaders, including the Earl of Salisbury, were killed by the townspeople of Cirencester. Around twenty-six others were executed.

The failure of this 'Epiphany Rising' sealed Richard's fate. The rising had demonstrated that there were compelling reasons finally to dispose of Richard and publicly demonstrate him to be dead. But there were also considerations against publicly executing him, if only because 'king-killing' might set a dangerous precedent.

The general view among contemporary chroniclers was that Richard was certainly dead by the middle of February 1400, and that he had possibly starved himself to death in Pontefract Castle. It may well be

Background

that Richard died of starvation, as his skeleton, when examined in the nineteenth century, showed no sign of violence, and the Percys, who were in an excellent position to know what happened in Pontefract, would claim later that the king had ordered Richard be starved to death – a process that took fifteen days.

But although Richard's body, its face exposed to public gaze, was exhibited in London before being buried at Kings Langley, King Henry IV was not to exorcize his predecessor so easily. In one form or another, the ghost of King Richard would haunt him for the rest of his days.

Uprising in Wales

Any hopes King Henry had that the death of Richard would ease pressure on him and establish the new regime more securely were quickly dampened. In September 1400 Henry mounted a major military expedition into Scotland in support of the Percys' ongoing campaign there. But the Scots declined to meet the massive invasion force in battle, adopting a 'scorched earth' strategy until the English were forced to withdraw.

And Henry soon faced an additional threat nearer home.

Although the last independent Welsh rulers had been crushed in 1283 by King Edward I and Wales brought under the English crown and the Marcher lords, even over a century later the Welsh remained dry tinder, which a spark was likely to ignite. There had been a major rebellion in 1294–1295, and several lesser outbreaks subsequently, while at the height of Edward III's campaigns in France, Owain Lawgoch, a descendant of the last Welsh princes, had presented a serious threat until killed by an English hired assassin.

Although troops recruited in Wales had made up a significant proportion of Edward's forces in France, large numbers of the Welsh people remained restive under their English overlords, while the partially Welsh ancestry of the Mortimers, among the greatest of the Marcher lords, made support in Wales for their claim to the English throne a potentially serious factor.

Edward I had attempted to cement English control of Wales by establishing a series of towns, usually associated with castles, which he populated with English settlers. Few of them flourished. The Welsh were excluded from the new towns, and could be punished by death if found within their walls after the evening curfew. They were denied trading rights and privileges, which were only granted to the English townspeople, and were forced to sell their own produce to the settlers on disadvantageous terms.

Perhaps because of this, the English settlements remained isolated and often paranoid outposts of alien rule. Even though by this time the rules against Welsh residents had been somewhat relaxed, in the minds of the settlers, and the government officials who were also based in them, they were surrounded by a hostile sea of Welshmen, and, although this view was at times exaggerated, by the latter part of the fourteenth century it still contained a good deal of truth.

Outside the immediate confines of the English settlements, the traditional Welsh way of life had been only superficially altered by the Edwardian conquest. When settlers brought in from England increasingly occupied the more fertile river valleys and narrow coastal plains, the dispossessed Welsh perforce established themselves in the harsher upland hills and moors. 'Welsh' Wales was a land of small villages and scattered farmsteads, where the raising of cattle, driven in great herds to sell as far afield as London, and to a lesser extent sheep-rearing, were the basis of the 'native' economy.

Although normally subject to English overlords, the native Welsh squirearchy ('uchelwyr') controlled many aspects of Welsh life, and were regarded by their Welsh tenantry, bound by ties of kinship and occasionally as the result of threats or actual violence, as their natural lords. The *uchelwyr*, although they had, in many cases, received an education in England and fought in the English armies in France and Scotland, remained fiercely wedded to the Welsh past, proud of their sometimes convoluted descent from the old Welsh royal dynasties, encouraged in this way of thought by the wandering bards and minstrels, who recalled the past glories of the Welsh people, and promised the return of King Arthur or the rise of a new leader who would regain Wales its freedom from the 'Saxon'.

The total population of Wales at the start of the fifteenth century was probably around a quarter of a million, reduced, as in other parts of the country, by the recent ravages of the 'Black Death'. There were

Background

two distinct systems of rule in Wales. Much of the east and south of the country, and much of the area just to the east of the rather vaguely defined Welsh border, was divided into around forty lordships, under the collective name of the 'Marches'. The Marcher lordships, originally consisting of territory granted to Anglo-Norman nobility on condition they conquered it from the Welsh, still had a considerable amount of autonomy, with their own legal and administrative systems. By far the largest of the Marcher lordships, extending through much of north-eastern and Central Wales, was held by the Mortimer family, closely followed in extent by the lands of the Arundel family.

The relationship between the Marcher lords and their Welsh subjects varied. Some of the smaller Marcher lordships had their owners in residence, which, depending on the character of the lord concerned, might affect relations with their tenants either favourably or otherwise. The larger lordships, however, were more often run by officials, usually English, whose dealings with the tenants were largely governed by the desire to extract as much in money or produce as they could. In these cases there was often a power vacuum waiting to be filled.

About a third of Wales – mainly the territory that had been conquered by Edward I in the north and west of the country – formed the 'Principality', and was a possession of the crown. Although both here and in the Marches, it was possible for the Welsh gentry to occupy minor and middle-ranking office, the higher posts were generally filled by Englishmen.

There was a similar situation with regard to the Church in Wales. Between 1372 and 1400, out of sixteen bishops, only one was Welsh. The alienation of the Welsh clergy, often providing vital leadership in the local communities, was a major factor in arousing discontent against English rule.

By 1400 Wales was a land of mounting unrest. Its population was divided into two increasingly polarized factions: on one side the English settlers, garrisons and administrators, with some of the minority of Welsh who had prospered under English rule, and on the other the bulk of the increasingly alienated 'native' Welsh population. The sense of bitterness and regret for the past among many of the Welsh was apparent: 'Where once there were Britons, we now have Englishmen; Welshmen suffer daily thereby.'

War for the Throne

The increasing demands of English landlords, themselves having to cope with the demographic and economic consequences of the 'Black Death', increased the disaffection. Coupled with this, the running down of the war with France lessened the opportunities for Welshmen to advance or enrich themselves by deeds of prowess, and was creating a reservoir of discontented veterans living in poorer circumstances at home in Wales.

The political turmoil at the end of the fourteenth century added to the sense of alarm and unease in Wales. The death of Roger Mortimer, Earl of March, in 1398, had left the great Mortimer lordships in the hands of a minor, inevitably followed by a lessening of firm government there. The relative favour shown to the Welsh by Richard II had raised hopes of an improvement in conditions, to be dashed by the 'revolution' of 1399.

All these discontents were fuelled by the Welsh love of mythology and yearning for a past, which although it had perhaps never quite existed, was potent in the Welsh national consciousness. Thus, by 1400, Wales was ripe for revolt, needing only a leader – and a spark – to ignite it. It found both in Owain Glyn Dwr.

Glyn Dwr was one of the wealthiest of the *uchelwyr*, and one of the few to hold his lands, mainly around Sycarth on the Welsh border near Oswestry, and Glyndyfrdwy, in the Dee valley near Corwen, directly from the crown. Significantly, in light of what was to follow, he could also claim descent from most of Wales' former royal dynasties. Details of Glyn Dwr's early life are scanty, but he was most probably born in 1359, making him just over 40 years of age in 1400. His upbringing conformed to the traditional pattern of contemporary English and Welsh gentry: his late childhood spent in the household of the Earl of Arundel, then several years of legal training at Westminster, followed by military service with Arundel, quite possibly including being present at Radcot Bridge in the forces of the Lords Appellant. He certainly served in Richard II's expedition to Scotland in 1385, his military prowess celebrated by the Welsh bards, and possibly in one or both of Richard's Irish expeditions. By the closing years of Richard's reign, Glyn Dwr was leading the life of a prosperous country landowner, his home and hospitality praised by his near-neighbour, the

Background

bard Iolo Goch. So far as he had any political sympathies, they were just as likely to have been with Henry as with Richard.

Yet in September 1400, when Wales at last flamed into open revolt, Glyn Dwr was at its head. The immediate cause seems to have been a dispute over land with Owain's powerful Marcher neighbour, Reginald, Lord Grey of Ruthin, who, unfortunately for Glyn Dwr, was a close associate of the new king. It was also said (though on uncertain grounds) that Grey deliberately withheld from Glyn Dwr a summons for him to join the Scottish expedition of 1400, and accused him of being a traitor.

In reality there were probably a number of reasons for what followed. Although he did not yet openly proclaim himself Prince of Wales, Owain was regarded as such by many of the 160 or so relatives and followers who met at Glyndyfrdwy on 16 September, and two days later, armed with bows, spears and swords, crossed the hills and sacked and burnt the town of Ruthin, on market day. From there they forged a trail of destruction across north-eastern Wales, burning and looting the towns of Denbigh, Flint, Harwarden, Holt and Rhuddlan, although, significantly, in every case the associated castle continued to hold out.

From Holt the insurgents headed south, their target the town of Welshpool on the River Severn. But here, not for the last time, the lightly-armed Welshmen found themselves outclassed by better trained and better equipped English forces, and were quickly scattered by a determined attack by the Sheriff of Shropshire, Hugh Burnell, reinforced by levies from Staffordshire and Warwickshire.

Nevertheless, the potential for serious trouble in Wales remained, Glyn Dwr was still at large, and in North Wales his Anglesey cousins, Rhys and Gwyllim ap Tudur, regarded as the leading Welsh military figures of the area, were now in arms.

News of the outbreak reached King Henry at Northampton. His advisers tended to minimize the severity of the threat, and the king evidently concluded that a *chevauchée*, or mounted punitive raid, would be sufficient to quell the outbreak. The levies of ten Midland shires were ordered to join him at Lichfield and Shrewsbury, and from here marched into North Wales, crossing the Menai Straits into Anglesey without serious opposition, although a detachment of his men was evidently worsted in a skirmish with the Tudurs near Beaumaris.

In reprisal, the king ordered the burning of the nearby friary at Llanfaes, and then led his forces back over the border to Shrewsbury. Having bared his teeth, so to speak, Henry now adopted a conciliatory stance, offering pardons to most of the leading rebels, excluding only a handful, including Glyn Dwr himself, whose estates were declared forfeit.

The king evidently hoped (and partly convinced himself) that his show of strength had achieved the desired effect. Certainly, as winter approached, although Glyn Dwr and a handful of followers were still at large in the mountains of North Wales, there was reason to hope that the uprising was a spent force. It is indeed possible that extending the pardon to include Glyn Dwr himself might have ended the rebellion.

But there were hardline forces on both sides which had no desire for reconciliation. It was reported that many Welsh labourers in England, and Welsh students at Oxford, were either secretly returning home to join the rebels, sending back money, or were in touch with irreconcilable Ricardian plotters in England.

When it met in January 1401, the English Parliament was in no mood to offer clemency. The rebellion had hardened the already strong anti-Welsh sentiment of many in England. In February the commons presented Henry with a series of anti-Welsh measures. Welshmen living in England and the Marches would be stripped of their entitlement to hold a large number of offices, including the constableships of castles. The people of a district would be held responsible for any breaches of the peace within their area, and would be liable personally for any felonies, robberies or trespasses. All criminals were to face English justice, instead of the old Welsh laws permitted to continue in some places. The Welsh were to pay for the upkeep and repair of castles and town walls in North Wales.

The problem for the English government lay in enforcing this new legislation, for, as spring approached, there were fears that Owain Glyn Dwr might soon resume his activities.

To co-ordinate operations against the rebels in North Wales, a council, under the nominal control of the 13-year-old Prince Henry,

Background

Chevauchée

A French term meaning 'promenade' or 'horse charge' used to describe raids designed to lay waste to enemy territory. It was intended to weaken the authority of an enemy regime or cause disaffection among its subjects – though often it had the opposite effect.

Generally associated with the English forces during the Hundred Years' War, the *chevauchée* had been used at least as far back as the Norman invasion of England in 1066. However, it was developed and refined during the campaigns of Edward III and the Black Prince. It utilized relatively small armies of fast-moving mounted troops. Taking booty and hostages, as well as causing destruction, were the primary objects of these raids.

Chevauchées were ideally suited to light horsemen or 'hobilars', who, as well as destroying crops and buildings, could also drive off livestock. Similar raids were used by the Scots in Northern England.

Some of the English *chevauchées* in France covered considerable distances. Perhaps the most famous, and destructive, was that mounted by the Black Prince in 1355. Leaving Bordeaux in the autumn with 5,000 mounted men, Edward devastated Angoulême and Armagnac, with the city of Toulouse as his apparent objective. In fact the English lacked the means to besiege the city and eventually returned to Bordeaux. A second large-scale raid the following year also failed to achieve any clear result.

Although villages and farmsteads would always remain vulnerable to *chevauchée*-style operations, French cities were gradually more strongly fortified, leading to a decline of the *chevauchée*.

Henry IV's use of the *chevauchée* in Wales had limited results, partly through lack of targets, and because the Welsh, like the French in the later years of the war, declined to offer battle in the open, contenting themselves with picking off stragglers.

was set up, based on Chester. Although the prince was regarded as being on the verge of manhood, he required an experienced adviser by his side. The Percys remained high in royal favour. The Earl of Northumberland had been made Constable of England, and

War for the Throne

Hotspur Warden of the East March of Scotland and Berwick, and Constable of Roxburgh Castle.

Early in 1401 Hotspur was appointed as Justice of North Wales, Justice of Chester and Constable of North Wales. Apart from in effect making him military commander in the area, Hotspur was also given stewardship of large areas of the Mortimer lordship, with his uncle, Thomas Percy, Earl of Worcester, being given similar powers in Central Wales.

There is no reason to think that Hotspur, who established his operational headquarters in the Mortimer castle at Denbigh, was reluctant to assume his new role. As uncle by marriage of the young Earl of March, he was an appropriate choice to administer part of his estates.

Despite the ordnances of the English Parliament, Hotspur had been given powers to continue the policy of clemency, which had hitherto been the hallmark of many of Henry's proceedings. However, Glyn Dwr himself, and a number of the other major participants in the rising of the previous autumn, were still excluded from pardon, and it was they who now rekindled the revolt.

The English still relied on the chain of castles constructed by Edward I from 1277 onwards, to contain any rebellion. And for the most part, they had had considerable success. Second only to the great fortress of Caernarvon in its impressive strength was Conwy Castle, commanding the crossing of the river of the same name, its white lime-washed walls dominating the associated English-inhabited town protected by its own strong walls.

Despite being strengthened after the outbreak of the rebellion, Conwy's garrison consisted only of fifteen men-at-arms and sixty archers, under the command of John Massey of Puddington, a highly experienced professional soldier from Cheshire, who had served both Richard and Henry, and whose father had died at Crécy.

Massey and his garrison should, in normal circumstances, have been strong enough to see off any attack that Rhys and Gwyllim ap Tudur would have been able to mount. He was, however, expecting any opponents to obey the generally accepted laws of war, which, among other things, forbade bloodshed on major religious festivals. So on Good Friday (1 April) Massey felt it safe to take all but two of his men for morning service in the parish church, which lay just outside the castle walls.

The Tudur brothers had no such scruples. A party of forty insurgents made their way stealthily to the foot of the castle rock, then one of their number, dressed as a carpenter, made his way to the castle gates and claimed to have been sent to carry out repairs. The two unsuspecting custodians opened the gates to give him entry. They were rushed by the hidden rebels, led by Gwyllim ap Tudur, and both were strangled. This method of killing was probably adopted both for its relative silence and as a way of being able to claim not to have shed blood in contravention of the Church's edicts. Conwy Castle was in Welsh hands.

Before entering the castle, Gwyllim and his men, aided by a larger force under Rhys ap Tudur, lurking in the wooded hills outside Conwy, had set part of the town ablaze. While the terrified townspeople and his own men tried to quell the blaze, a humiliated and angry Massey sent word of the disaster to Hotspur.

The Tudurs, as they would have been aware, had no prospect of holding Conwy Castle indefinitely – such was not their aim. Their plan was to use the castle as a bargaining counter with which to obtain the pardons from which they had been excluded.

For Hotspur the loss of Conwy Castle was a major humiliation. Its fortifications and great store of provisions meant that it was unlikely to be retaken except by means of a costly and prolonged siege. And for as long as the castle remained in Welsh hands, it would serve as a symbol likely to kindle further acts of rebellion.

Hotspur, at the head of 120 mounted men-at-arms and 300 archers, rode at once to Conwy. Massey was dismissed from his command, had his lands forfeited, and was put under arrest.

None of this brought recovery of the castle any closer, and a month later Hotspur was still tied down blockading the castle and attempting to protect the town of Conwy from raids by Rhys ap Tudur and his men, who still lurked in the neighbourhood. Although he wrote to the king on 4 May that he hoped the rebels would be 'well chastised', Hotspur believed that some sort of deal with the Tudurs was inevitable if the siege were not to drag on into the summer. However, when negotiations began, Welsh proposals were unacceptable to the

War for the Throne

king, with the Tudurs demanding free pardons for themselves and all their men, and that none of them should be put on trial before the town's court. Eventually a compromise was reached, and the terms sent to the king for approval. Henry was far from happy, writing to Prince Henry that the suggested terms were 'not at all honourable to us, but a matter of the most evil precedent'.

But talks continued, and early in June a rather shabby agreement was reached between Gwyllim ap Tudur and Hotspur, by which the castle was surrendered. About nine of the defenders were seized by their companions as they slept, tied up and handed over to the besiegers. Gwyllim and the remainder of his men were allowed to go free, while their companions were hanged, drawn and quartered. The chronicler Adam of Usk wrote of the surrender of Conwy Castle:

> on the 28th of May next following the Welsh surrendered the said Castle, cowardly for themselves and treacherously for their comrades. For having bound twelve of their number who were very hateful to the prince, by stealth as they slept after the night watches, they gave them up on condition of saving their own and others' lives. And the nine thus bound and yielded up to the prince they straight away saw them drawn, disembowelled, hanged, beheaded, and quartered.

The Siege of Conwy had been an episode reflecting little credit on any of those involved. Indeed, it is tempting to think that Hotspur, with his highly developed sense of chivalry, must have resented being forced into such a discreditable solution. More significantly, the long-drawn-out operations at Conwy had tied down large numbers of English troops, and given Glyn Dwr much-needed time to rekindle his revolt.

On 3 May Hotspur had been reporting optimistically to the king's council that the bulk of the dissidents in Caernarvonshire and Merioneth had now submitted, but that his own shortage of funds was critical:

> those rebels who are in the castles of Conway and Rhys [ap Tudur], which is in the mountains [...] I hope will be well

Background

chastised, if God pleases, by the forces and authorities, which my redoubtable brother the Prince [Henry] has sent there, as well of his counsel as of his retinue, to hold the siege before the rebels in the said castles; which siege if it can be continued until the said rebels are taken, will be a great ease and comfort to the governance of this country in time to come [...] the peasantry of the said country of North Wales, that is to say the counties of Caernarvon and Merioneth, have just presented themselves before me and humbly thanked my redoubtable brother, the Prince, for his very great kindness in supplicating our lord the King for his gracious pardon, and they humbly beg for the confirmation of this under his seal, offering to give him of their own will (beside the usual dues) and without any other request, as great a sum as they gave to King Richard when he was King and Prince [...] and you will remember how many times I have besought you for the payment of the soldiers of the king in the City of Berwick and the East Marches of England, who are in such great poverty that they cannot bear arms for the want of their pay, and for them you are supplicated to order that they be paid in manner as was promised between the Treasurer and myself at our last meeting, if better payment cannot be obtained for them. For otherwise I must come to you for the said payment, everything else being of minor importance [...] [But] the great want and necessity I saw in all the country, in good faith, are so insupportable that I cannot bear them any longer than the end of the month, three or four days longer ...

Lack of financial support from the king would eventually become a festering source of grievance for the Percys, who would come to see the neglect as deliberate malice. In fact, the situation facing Henry was more complex. Royal demands for money had been a major factor in the opposition to Richard I, and was not a policy that Henry wished to imitate. He had already spent some £60,000 (roughly £3,250,000 in present-day terms) in largely fruitless operations in Scotland and Wales, and Parliament was reluctant to grant further taxes until Henry made concessions regarding the councillors he had appointed. Even

War for the Throne

Siege Warfare

A fifteenth-century siege of a major castle or well-fortified town was a considerable undertaking, requiring a large number of troops with significant resources. Basically, sieges could take one or more of three main forms: assault (with or without bombardment) and mining (which could also be employed separately) or blockade (aimed at starving the defenders into surrender).

A blockade was cheapest in terms of casualties and equipment, but could take a considerable time, and there was often the possibility of a relief force coming to the assistance of the garrison. The aim of blockade and starvation was normally to bring the defenders to seek terms, and sometimes – if the garrison commander's aim was to save face rather than fight to the last – a few shots were enough to satisfy his honour before yielding.

Siege equipment was always cumbersome and difficult to move. A trebuchet (most effective of the siege engines) might require a team of wagons pulled by up to sixty oxen to move it while disassembled. Guns were slightly easier to transport but required large quantities of ammunition.

Assault was normally only employed against small or inadequately defended garrisons, and might be expected to be bloody and costly for all involved.

then, his tax collectors met with violent opposition in many parts of the country, at least one being murdered.

It was partly because of these difficulties, as well as from a feeling that the trouble and expense involved in recovering Conwy had been largely the result of Hotspur's constable losing it in the first place, which led to an unsympathetic response from the king to Percy's pleas.

In Wales itself, Hotspur was trying unsuccessfully to track down the illusive Glyn Dwr in the wild uplands of Merioneth, although he received some satisfaction from a minor victory gained by John Charlton of Powys over a rebel force in Central Wales, but Hotspur was unable, or unwilling, to follow up this success. On 4 June he was telling the royal council that unless he was provided with funds – he claimed to be owed £5,000 – he would have to leave Wales 'which becomes a matter of necessity to me, for I cannot bear the costs I am at, then the complete success of the rebels is assured'.

Around the same time there is evidence suggesting Hotspur was in touch with Glyn Dwr himself. The Welsh leader was still apparently receptive to peace feelers, if a full pardon could be guaranteed. Hotspur and Glyn Dwr may have met during the Scottish campaign of 1385 and if they did not meet face to face in the spring of 1401, there were certainly exchanges of messages between them regarding Glyn Dwr's possible submission. Suggestions that they also discussed overthrowing King Henry are almost certainly premature, but links were established that could be activated later. Once again the king's council was opposed to granting Glyn Dwr any terms, and indeed went so far as to suggest Hotspur lure the Welsh leader into a trap and then kill him. Hotspur, already uneasy after the terms agreed at Conwy, angrily rejected the idea, saying that 'it was not in keeping with his rank to use the oath of fealty as a means of deception'.

Believing himself blamed for the loss of Conwy, Hotspur wrote to the king's council:

> as to what is written in your said letters that I do well and safely guard all the castles, which I have in keeping for the term of my life or otherwise, in the said parts, so that from my negligence no pillage, damage or other loss happen either to the castles or the country [...] I am charged upon pain of forfeiting the said castles and the profits appertaining thereto without ever having been restored or admitted to the keeping of them. I wish you to know that I have not in Wales any castle of my keeping for which I cannot answer and will not answer for.

In June Hotspur made a final plea to the king:

> I see much pillage and mischief in the country, that good and hasty measures ought to be immediately adopted by sea as well as by land. All the country is without doubt in great peril of being destroyed by the rebels if I should leave before the arrival of my successor, the which [sic] will be an affair of necessity; for I cannot bear the cost that I am put to without ordering from

you. And touching this that has been done by my very honoured uncle [Thomas Percy, Earl of Worcester] and other forces in his company, I hope that this has been certified unto you and of my doing this by land and sea for my soldiers' pay and my own expenses, and for the journey I had on the 13th May last to Cader Idris, God be Praised. The bearer John Irby was with me and can acquaint you with the details. Sir Hugh Browe was with me with twelve lances and one hundred archers of my right honourable cousin the Earl of Arundel, without any other aid, at my proper charges; and by such governance as you may see meet to order for this answer [...] and please to know that news have reached me this day from the lord of Powys, as to his combat with Owain Glyn Dwr, whom he hath discomfited, and wounded many of his men on his way to my much honoured uncle and myself as he certified, for which I thank God.

By July he had left his Welsh command and was back in the north, organizing preparations to meet an expected Scottish attack. While Hotspur was not yet estranged from the Lancastrian regime, it was clear that his relations with Henry – always uneasy following the latter's seizure of the throne – had taken a turn for the worse.

By now Glyn Dwr had begun spreading his rebellion to other parts of Wales, sending out letters to likely supporters. He told Henry Don of Kidwelly:

We inform you that we hope to be able, by God's help and yours, to deliver the Welsh people from the captivity of our English enemies who, for a long time now elapsed, have oppressed us and our ancestors. And you may know from your own perception that now their time draws to a close and because, according to God's ordnance from the beginning success turns towards us, no one need doubt that a good issue will result, unless it be lost through sloth and strife.

It was a message calculated to appeal both to Welsh grievances and their belief in prophecy and divine support. Even in England, especially among the Welsh students at Oxford, unrest was growing.

Background

Though much of this amounted to no more than words, there was evidence that men were being recruited in Oxford to go back to Wales to fight for Glyn Dwr, and that money was being raised for his cause.

With the bulk of the English forces concentrated in North Wales, Glyn Dwr now carried the rebellion into the previously quiet south. He established a base for 'Plant Owain' – 'Owain's Children' – as his men were known to the Welsh, in the area around Plynlimmon, in the central uplands of Wales, from where he could strike north, south and east.

With most available English troops still holding down North Wales, it was left to the community of Flemish settlers of south-west Wales to raise a force of some 1,500 men to meet Glyn Dwr. Glyn Dwr himself was said to have only 400 men immediately available, but in an action in the Hyddegen valley, 2 miles from Plynlimmon, after a fierce fight, completely routed the enemy:

> In summer Owen rose with 120 reckless men and robbers and he brought them in warlike fashion to the uplands of Ceredigion; and 1,500 men of the lowlands of Ceredigion and of Rhos and Penfro assembled there and came to the mountain with the intent to seize Owen. The encounter between them was on Hyddgant Mountain, and no sooner did the English troops turn their backs in flight than 200 of them were slain. Owen now won great fame, and a great number of youths and fighting men from every part of Wales rose and joined him, until he had a great host at his back.

Hyddegen was the victory Glyn Dwr had needed to give his movement credibility. It also seems to have been the event that convinced him of the righteousness of his cause. Henceforward he would fly the banner depicting the four lions of the Royal House of Gwynedd, and begin to style himself Prince of Wales. And from now on his 'Children' began to wage war with a new ruthlessness, burning and killing wherever they went along the borders of Central Wales. Once again they were checked at Welshpool, but only after the town had gone up in flames.

By September a reluctant King Henry was forced to prepare another major military expedition into Wales. On 18 September, having secured funds from a grudging Parliament (which had been forced to acknowledge mounting threats from France and Scotland, as well as Wales), Henry summoned the Midland levies to meet him at Worcester on 1 October.

The expedition lasted a fortnight and was a total failure. Beset by foul weather and with no sign of the illusive Glyn Dwr, Henry and his troops blundered around in the hills of Central Wales, led astray by a Welsh guide, Llywellyn ap Gruffydd Vychan, who after two days defiantly told the king: 'I have two sons serving with Glyn Dwr and I will on no account reveal his counsels which will prove so penal to you.' He was hung, drawn and quartered by the furious Henry. But Glyn Dwr remained out of reach. His irregular fighters from time to time appeared out of the mist and rain to harry detachments and stragglers from the English army, on one occasion capturing the horses, tents and armour of the young Prince Henry.

The king's response was to sack and burn the great Cistercian monastery of Strata Florida, beloved of the Welsh people because eleven of their princes were buried there. The king's horses were stabled in the abbey church and its treasures carried off when the army left. It was an act of 'frightfulness' rather than logical strategy, and within days Henry was back in England, at Hereford, with nothing to show for his efforts but 1,000 terrified Welsh children, brought back as hostages.

A triumphant Glyn Dwr now swung north, and, somewhat optimistically, attempted to surprise the great castle of Caernarvon. A sally by the garrison, supported by armed townsmen, repulsed the attack, claiming to have killed 300 of the rebels.

As winter drew on, there seems to have been a final attempt to end the rebellion by compromise. Significantly, it was the Earl of Northumberland who presented Glyn Dwr's case to Prince Henry and his council at Chester:

> May it please you to know that envoys have come from Owain Glyn Dwr telling me that the said Owain wishes to parley with representatives of my people, upon which I sent him to know his intent, saying that if he would submit without conditions to the

Background

Armour

The early years of the fifteenth century were a time of transition in the types of armour in use. The impact of the war bow in the hands of skilled archers was leading to the development of full plate armour, but it would be some years before this came into wide use.

Most of the men-at-arms engaged in the battles examined here would have worn a mixture of plate and mail. Typical features were the mail hauberk, or coat, an aventail under the helmet, and a bascinet-style helmet, which often, though not always, had a visor fitted. Plate armour might protect the arms and shins and feet, and articulated steel gauntlets would be worn. Shields were probably not widely used by men fighting on foot. There would have been little or no difference in the armour of men-at-arms in the English, Scottish or Welsh armies.

---

mercy of our Lord the King, I would make it my task to beg for his life, without promising him anything. He has replied that he dare not come for anything to England because he has heard that the commons of England have slain some great lords against the wishes of the king our lord without being brought to justice. And he made other demands and requests of no consequence.

Glyn Dwr was referring to the killings of those involved in the 'Epiphany Plot' of 1400. The message is of the more significance in confirming that a channel of communication was now open between Glyn Dwr and the Percys. It may be that nothing was discussed other than what was stated in Northumberland's letter to Prince Henry, but the earl could equally have been covering himself in the knowledge that word of his contacts with Glyn Dwr would reach royal ears from other sources.

Once again King Henry seemed mindful to open negotiations with Glyn Dwr. But his inclinations were overruled by the royal council, which held that 'it neither was nor could be honourable and befitting the king's majesty to remit such a malefactor his offence'.

War for the Throne

It would prove to be the last slim chance for a compromise. By November, Glyn Dwr was in touch with King Robert III of Scotland and various Irish chieftains, calling on them for support against a common enemy: 'I humbly beseech you, kneeling upon my knees, that it may please your royal majesty to send unto me a certain number of men-at-arms who may aid me and may withstand with God's help mine and your foes aforesaid.'

Ahead lay a deepening and bitter struggle.

The Armies

The opposing armies involved in the struggle for the throne during the first decade of the fifteenth century had common characteristics and marked differences. We will look at each in turn, starting with the English armies of Henry IV.

The English Army

There were significant differences between English armies that fought in France (for example) and those that campaigned on mainland Britain. For several hundred years, the mainstay of armies raised for service within the royal dominions in Britain had been the militia. The militia, or *posse comitatus*, theoretically made the entire male population between the ages of 15 and 60 liable for service. Their liability, however, was only for campaigning within the royal domains. English kings tended to claim that these included Wales and Scotland, although this was sometimes disputed by local communities, which had the responsibility of mustering, arming, equipping, and maintaining for forty days the levies they were ordered to raise. After this time, responsibility for their upkeep theoretically rested with the crown, though in practice – particularly when the cash-strapped King Henry was involved – such funding did not always materialize. It was also one reason for the short duration of his campaigns, because of his desire to discharge the militia before such upkeep became necessary.

There was a recognized system for raising the militia. The crown would select which counties were to be summoned: in the case of the Shrewsbury campaign and the operations against Glyn Dwr, these were normally the Midlands counties. Each county had a number of

Background

Commissioners of Array – most often local knights. The king would send them and the sheriff a quota of the total number of men he expected their county to provide. The commissioners in turn would give each local community the number of men required from them, and responsibility for raising these would lie with the village constables and local justices of the peace or gentry.

It was a system with considerable potential for corruption and evasion. No community was eager to part with the most able-bodied and economically useful of its members, for an unknown period of time, with the possibility that they might never return at all. So there was a tendency to attempt to unload undesirables, the less fit, or even passing strangers. In theory the commissioners were to hold 'musters' to check on the quality of men presented, before despatching them to the stipulated rendezvous by a required date. But the commissioners themselves were liable to come under local pressure and their readiness to comply might also be affected by the current popularity of the regime. Desertion was also a significant factor and it has been calculated that, on average, only between a half and two-thirds of those summoned would actually appear.

The standard of equipment and the training of the militia also varied widely. In some areas, such as Cheshire with its long-standing military tradition, militiamen were generally of good quality. In other less martial areas, the standard was much lower.

Each individual was supposed to be armed and equipped to a required standard based on his economic position in the community. The requirement might vary from hauberk, sword, knife and horse for a better-off man down to a sword and a knife for the poorest. Bows were to be carried whenever possible.

Again, the percentage of archers and their level of experience varied considerably. Throughout the fourteenth and fifteenth centuries government decrees were issued banning the playing of 'idle games' such as quoits and football, and stipulating that all those liable for service with the militia should practice archery at the butts on Sundays and holy days. But how regularly and conscientiously this was observed is impossible to say. In general, the militia of the northern counties seems to have included a higher proportion of archers than those elsewhere.

War for the Throne

By the start of the fifteenth century increasing use was being made of the 'indenture' or contract system, whereby an individual magnate or captain would agree to provide the king with a stipulated number of troops for an agreed period in return for payment. This system was supposed to be used in all overseas campaigns and was increasingly adopted at home. So in practice, a typical English army might consist of a mixture of household troops of the king and his magnates (usually professional soldiers), a number of indentured companies, and a varying number of militia.

There is some uncertainty as to how these elements were actually organized. There is no evidence that individual retinues were combined in any further way, and it seems probable that each of the three main divisions of an army – the 'vaward', main battle and rear – comprised a large number of smaller units and retinues, making command and control somewhat problematical.

Discipline also varied and was generally difficult to impose, especially when serving in areas close to home, as militiamen might easily desert and seek concealment in their local community. There were penalties for theft and unauthorized looting, and for molestation of women and desecration of churches. But, particularly in the Welsh campaigns, destruction of buildings and resources by burning was a recognized part of English strategy, and, even if commanders had been inclined to exempt those they viewed as rebels from the excesses of their men, in practice this would have been difficult.

Many men were attracted to war. In the case of knights and nobles the motivation was chivalry and military glory. But that said, all ranks went to war hoping for booty or other material gain. King Henry's wars provided little opportunity for this. Wales was a poor country and once a 'scorched earth' strategy had been carried out, there was little left worth taking.

As the enemy – in the case of the Welsh and various English opponents – were regarded as rebels and liable to punishment for treason, there was also no hope of financial gain through the payment of ransoms. The king was also at times reluctant to ransom his own men captured by the Welsh, partly on the grounds that he was unwilling to do anything to finance Glyn Dwr's war effort. This, of course, did nothing to foster enthusiasm.

Background

One of the major difficulties that hindered Henry's war effort was supplying his troops. Huge quantities of food, for both horses and men, were needed. For Henry's brief campaigns, the sheriffs of the counties that provided men also had to provide their upkeep, and in emergencies like the Percy rebellion of 1403, it may be assumed that the 'tally' system was used, whereby supplies were in effect requisitioned, in return for a tally that, in theory, could be redeemed with the royal exchequer at a later date.

In the later stages of the rebellion the prolonged siege operations required to regain the castles of Aberystwyth and Harlech made a more organized system of supply necessary. Merchants in Bristol and elsewhere were contracted to provide the soldiers with supplies, which were transported by sea.

The Scottish Army

There were a number of differences between the Scottish army at Homildon Hill and its English opponents. The bulk of the Scottish were feudal levies, raised in much the same way, and on similar terms. On the whole they were less well-equipped than their English counterparts.

Although the Scots had some archers, they were fewer in number and apparently less well trained than the English. The bulk of the Scottish levies were armed with long spears varying in length from 12–18 feet and, usually, a sword. Defensive armour normally comprised a 'jack' and bascinet-style helmet. Scottish knights and men-at-arms were armed and equipped in similar style to their English counterparts but were significantly fewer in number.

The bulk of Scottish troops were mounted, making them highly mobile. An early fourteenth-century writer, Jean le Bel wrote that:

> When they cross the border they advance sixty to seventy miles in a day and night, which would seem astonishing to anyone ignorant of their customs. The explanation is that, on their expeditions into England, they all come on horseback, except the irregulars who follow on foot. The knights and squires are mounted on fine, strong horses and the commoners on small ponies. Because they

have to pass over the wild hills of Northumberland, they bring no baggage carts.

Scottish spearmen usually operated in densely packed bodies, several ranks deep, known as 'schiltrons', which, although fairly manoeuvrable, provided easy targets for archers.

The Welsh Armies

A couple of centuries earlier, Welsh forces had been noted for their use of spearmen, probably similar to those employed by the Scots. By the time of the Glyn Dwr revolt, however, after many years forming part of the English forces in France, Welsh soldiers were mostly armed and equipped in the same fashion. And Glyn Dwr's forces included a significant number of archers.

The Welsh laboured under similar disadvantages to the Scots so far as men-at-arms were concerned. Although Welsh gentry such as Glyn Dwr himself were armed and equipped in the same way as English contemporaries they formed proportionately a much smaller part of the Welsh forces.

Many of Glyn Dwr's men were peasant levies, equipped with whatever weapons were available – mainly spears and swords with little protective armour, except sometimes a helmet and 'jack'. They were evidently poorly trained and ill-disciplined, and were unable to face English men-at-arms in open combat.

Pilleth and Homildon Hill

The year 1402 dawned ominously for King Henry. In an age when much weight was placed on signs and portents, the sight of a fiery comet sweeping across the night skies of Western Europe was widely regarded as extremely menacing. In England, a chronicler wrote:

> in the third year of King Henry's reign, there was a star seen in the firmament, which showed itself throughout all the world for diverse tokenings that should befall soon after. The star was named and called by the clergy Stella Comata.

But Henry had more earthly problems to consider. Most of the high hopes with which his reign had commenced had been dashed.

Background

In nearly every area problems were mounting rapidly. As well as complaining of the burden of high taxation, his subjects were also still suffering from the effects of increasing shortage of food caused by rises in the price of corn. There was once again evidence of renewed plotting by Ricardian supporters. There were rumours of plots to kill Henry and his sons. Meanwhile, conspirators (particularly numerous among the friars and other clergy) fomented discontent in King Richard's name. Several were questioned personally by Henry, and continued to proclaim their loyalty to Richard and their belief that he was still alive, even as they were taken away to execution.

In Wales, Glyn Dwr's rebels remained defiant. With the failure of the tentative peace talks of the autumn, the actions of both sides were becoming increasingly savage. In the late summer of 1401 Glyn Dwr's followers had stormed the castle at New Radnor. Some three-score of the captured garrison were lined up in the courtyard and beheaded. This may have been intended as a deliberate act of 'terror' to intimidate other enemies in the Welsh Marches. By now, raids by 'Owain's Children' were thrusting ever deeper into England. Western Shropshire, and even the suburbs of Hereford, were subject to attack by Welsh raiders. The great Edwardian castles of Aberystwyth and Harlech, virtually impossible to relieve by land, were beginning to come under pressure and could only be supplied by sea. And Glyn Dwr's cause was about to receive a major boost.

In April, Owain captured his greatest enemy, Lord Grey of Ruthin. Details of how this was accomplished are unclear. However, it appears that the Welsh launched a minor attack on Ruthin, which provoked Grey, with a detachment of the garrison, to make an incautious sally. The English force ran into an ambush in nearby woods. Grey was surrounded and captured and taken away to imprisonment near Glyn Dwr's estate at Glyndyfrdwy, then to Snowdonia, while negotiations for his ransom began. King Henry proved much more ready to find means for the release of his friend than he had seemingly been willing to exert himself in the cause of providing Hotspur with adequate funds. A commission was set up to negotiate with the Welsh on the terms for Grey's release. Welsh demands were high. Eventually, a ransom of 10,000 marks was agreed, of which 6,000 were to be paid within a month. Grey's eldest son would replace his father as a hostage until the remainder of the ransom was paid. The demands were met with the assistance of the king but Lord Grey would be financially embarrassed for many years to come.

With their principal enemy in their hands, the Welsh rebels were able to range freely across much of North Wales. The cathedral town of St Asaph was their first target. Here, the cathedral itself and a number of clergymen's houses were set alight and destroyed. Glyn Dwr's men also struck at Harlech. A major expedition, consisting of 400 archers and 100 men-at-arms, had to be despatched from Chester to relieve the beleaguered outpost. There were also unfounded rumours of a Scottish fleet operating off the Welsh coast. The hard-pressed citizens of Chester were ordered to finance several ships to counter this threat.

From the beginning of the year, the English government began to reorganize its defences in Wales. Hotspur returned from the north to resume command in North Wales, and Thomas Percy, Earl of Worcester, took over in South Wales. Although the south had hitherto been unaffected by the rebellion, orders were given for the strengthening of a number of garrisons in that area. The castles at Kidwelly and Monmouth were to be repaired and the number of men in several garrisons increased.

Hotspur evidently returned briefly from the north of England to organize renewed measures to suppress the rebellion. Percy was able to resupply the castles of Denbigh and Ruthin, but was able to achieve little more. It should have been clear that only a major military expedition, striking at several points simultaneously, was likely to put an end to the rebellion. But lack of resources made this impracticable. Only one expedition was actually launched in the spring of 1402 and that would meet with a major disaster.

Pilleth

With the Earl of March still underage and effectively in royal custody, management of his estates was vested in his uncle, 26-year-old Sir Edmund Mortimer. There is no evidence that Mortimer had any significant previous military experience but he was the natural choice to command a force raised largely from among the Mortimer tenants. By this time, Welsh forces, possibly commanded by Glyn Dwr himself

Background

(although this is not certain), had moved down from Snowdonia and, no doubt reinforced by local sympathizers, were operating in Central Wales, especially in the area known as Maelienydd, which was Mortimer territory. Here they continued their customary tactics of burning and destroying churches, minor strongholds and villages, looting them and killing or driving away their inhabitants. It was a challenge to his authority that Sir Edmund Mortimer could not ignore.

The final spur, which forced him to take action, may have been when the Welsh sacked the town of Knighton, only a few miles from the major Mortimer strongholds of Ludlow and Wigmore. Mortimer's response was to call out 'almost all the militia of Herefordshire'. These were reinforced by his own household troops and various minor local gentry and their followers. The size of Mortimer's force has often been exaggerated – certainly by contemporary chroniclers – but Edmund probably had no more than 2,000 men, possibly considerably fewer. With him were at least four knights: Sir Walter Devereux of Weobley and Lyonshall, Sir Robert Whitney of Whitney on Wye, a former Sheriff of Herefordshire, Sir Kinnard de la Bere of Kinnerseley Castle, near Weobley and Sir Thomas Clanvowe of Pychard Cusop and Hergest. Each of these men will have brought their own retainers and tenants. One potential problem that faced Mortimer was how far he could depend upon his men. Some were Welsh and it was unclear if they could be relied upon to fight against their fellow countrymen. In previous centuries, Welsh troops had been employed in large numbers in English campaigns in Wales. But these had generally been directed against unpopular Welsh leaders such as Llywellyn ap Gruffydd in 1282, or against opponents already clearly doomed to defeat. Whether they would be willing to fight against an enemy who seemed to be riding the high tide of success was much less certain.

It is unclear whether Glyn Dwr himself was in command of the Welsh forces in the area. Some accounts suggest that Rhys Gethin ('the Fierce') of Crom Llanarch in the Conwy valley, one of Glyn Dwr's senior lieutenants, was actually in charge. Given that Welsh forces tended to be widely dispersed, it is quite possible that Glyn Dwr himself was elsewhere. In any event, the Welsh rebels who would encounter Mortimer were probably fewer in number than their opponents.

War for the Throne

Welsh scouts and sympathizers were almost certainly reporting Mortimer's movements to the rebel leader from the moment the English left Ludlow. It is equally likely, the deeper Mortimer and his men penetrated Welsh territory, that a hostile local population gave them little or no information regarding the activities of the enemy.

It must have been with increasing unease that Mortimer and his men advanced into difficult terrain, ideally suiting the guerrilla tactics favoured by 'Owain's Children'. It was an area of steep-sided valleys covered with oak woods. The narrow valley bottoms were frequently swampy and the roads and tracks few and usually in poor condition.

Contemporary accounts vary regarding the exact location of the Welsh forces when Mortimer began his march. According to one version the Welsh initially went to Knighton. In another account, they took position on high ground above the village of Pilleth, immediately upon learning Mortimer had quit Ludlow. The route Mortimer followed is also unclear, there being several possibilities. Sir Edmund may initially have gone to his stronghold at Wigmore, in order to pick up reinforcements. From there he may have marched over the hills to Lingen and from thence via Kinsham to Stapleton Norton. Alternatively, he may have marched directly from Ludlow by way of Richards Castle to Shobdon, and then via Rodd to Presteigne. Here he would have had to ford the River Lugg, and the dangers of having to cross the river – possibly in the face of an enemy attack – may have inclined him to take the route by Wigmore. There is a third possibility that the English troops may have entered Wales at Knighton and Brampton Bryan, as there is a local tradition of skirmishing in that area.

Mortimer and his men probably spent the night of 21 June near Whitton, and it would have been sometime the following morning when they came in sight of the enemy awaiting them on Bryn Glas Hill, just to the west of Pilleth. The Welsh position was naturally strong. Bryn Glas Hill has steep eastern slopes, which Mortimer would have had no alternative but to scale in order to get to grips with the enemy in the face of concentrated archery. Much of the hillside was apparently open ground, although there appears to have been some woods at its edge, with a narrow valley to the left of the hill, also thickly wooded.

Background

The strength of the Welsh army is uncertain. Although Glyn Dwr or Rhys Gethin had probably brought a small contingent from Snowdonia, they had probably been joined by other rebels from the immediate area where they were now operating. Perhaps there were around 1,500 Welsh facing Mortimer. Some of the best – mainly men-at-arms and spearmen – seem to have been placed in ambush in the valley to the left of Bryn Glas Hill. The remainder of the opposing forces were probably arrayed in orthodox fashion, with the archers formed up across the front of the men-at-arms and levies.

The battle may have opened with an archery exchange, but this probably did not continue for long because Mortimer, with only half the enemy forces visible to him, almost certainly believed he had superiority in numbers. In any case, with his less-than-enthusiastic levies galled by an archery barrage from the enemy, he had little choice but to take the offensive.

Most likely pulling back his own archers onto either flank, Mortimer and his army advanced up the hill towards the enemy. They continued to suffer from the effects of the Welsh archers, and the steep ascent of Bryn Glas doubtless disordered and fatigued them. Even as the English closed with Glyn Dwr's main body, the Welsh sprang their ambush, the concealed men-at-arms in the valley striking the English left flank. It appears that a considerable number of Mortimer's Welsh archers now switched sides, and, most probably throwing down their bows, attacked their erstwhile comrades in both flank and rear.

The effect on Mortimer's raw and poorly motivated troops was catastrophic. Although Mortimer and his knights fought desperately, the bulk of his levies broke ranks and routed down the hill towards the valley of the River Lugg below. Hotly pursued by the victorious Welsh, they were cut down and massacred in large numbers. Up to 1,100 of Mortimer's men may have died in the brief encounter on Bryn Glas. Among the dead were Robert Whitney, Kinnard de la Bere and Walter Devereux. Sir Edmund Mortimer himself was taken captive.

English chroniclers were horrified, not only by the defeat, but by the alleged atrocities performed on the dead and wounded by Welsh-women – presumably Glyn Dwr's camp followers. The description by one chronicler, John Capgrave, was particularly graphic. He wrote that 'After the battle full shamefully, the Welshwomen cut off men's members and put them in their mouths.' Another chronicler, Hollinshead, writing some forty years after the battle, gave more details:

> the shameful villainy used by the Welshwomen towards the dead carcasses were such as honest ears would be ashamed to hear and continent tongues to speak thereof. The dead bodies might not be buried without great sums of money being given for liberty to convey them away.

Modern historians have cast doubt on these allegations, saying there was no tradition of such atrocities being carried out in Welsh warfare. On the other hand, the fighting in the Welsh Marches was becoming steadily bitterer, and the possibility that some of the English dead may have been so treated cannot be ruled out. Many of the dead were buried in the river valley and others in grave pits near Pilleth Church.

A number of prisoners were taken, among them Thomas Clanvow, best known as the author of the poem, 'The Cuckoo and the Nightingale'. He was apparently well treated and ransomed four months later. But Sir Edmund Mortimer was a much more valuable prize, not to be surrendered lightly. His capture left the Mortimer lands on the Welsh border effectively leaderless. Furthermore, as uncle to one of the claimants to the English throne, Mortimer was an important political prize.

King Henry's response was both prompt and furious. In his beleaguered situation, the king was becoming increasingly suspicious of those around him. He already had some grounds to suspect the loyalty of the Mortimers. It was significant that ever since the negotiations between Glyn Dwr and Hotspur, the Mortimer lands in North Wales, centred on Denbigh, had largely been spared from Welsh attack. Rumours quickly grew that Mortimer was a not-entirely-unwilling prisoner – even that he had betrayed his own army.

It may be doubted Mortimer would in fact have sacrificed so many of his own followers for less than clear political ends. In any case, in some ways his capture suited King Henry rather well. For as long as Mortimer remained in Welsh hands, the potential opposition to the king from the Mortimer family was largely neutralized.

Background

Whether the king actively opposed Mortimer being ransomed is also unclear. His first response to the news of the disaster at Pilleth was to order immediate preparations for a massive punitive expedition into Wales, designed to end the threat from Glyn Dwr once and for all.

This time, three large armies, provisioned for fifteen days, were to strike simultaneously into Wales: one advancing from Hereford, one from Shrewsbury (led by the king in person), while the third army, advancing into North Wales from Chester, was to be under the nominal command of the 15-year-old Prince Henry.

The king was at Berkhamstead Castle in Berkshire when he learnt of Mortimer's defeat. On 25 June, he sent orders to his council that

> the Welsh rebels have captured Edmund Mortimer and several other knights, and the king wishes to proceed against the rebels himself. Warrant for orders under the privy seal to all the lords, knights and squires of his retinue, and to all those who have annuities from him, to be at Lichfield on 7 July armed and ready to make war in Wales.

In fact, it was not until 2 September that the three English armies at last began their advance.

By then the English position in Wales had deteriorated further. Glyn Dwr's men followed up their success at Pilleth by driving deep into Herefordshire and burning the town of Leominster. News of their victory – the most significant yet of the rebellion – spread rapidly across Wales and led to an upsurge in support for Glyn Dwr. The men of the Mortimer estates on the Welsh border flocked to the rebel cause. Other areas, such as Flintshire, previously unaffected by the uprising, also turned to Glyn Dwr. Some bands of 'Owain's Children' may have penetrated South Wales, threatening English garrisons such as Newport, Usk and Cardiff.

In mid and South Wales, absent Marcher lords were ordered to return to their estates to co-ordinate their defences. But in North Wales, the situation had deteriorated too far for this to have any effect. Large areas were now effectively out of English control. That said, English officials were still able to collect taxes until the end of the year in some areas, such as Anglesey. Thus the king and his advisers could still cling to the hope that a massive demonstration of military strength might dampen the flames of rebellion.

However, the triple-pronged invasion of Wales proved a major disaster. The king's own expedition marched from Shrewsbury up the valley of the River Severn and then across the Berwyn Mountains north-west into the Conwy valley. Here the English burnt the small town of Llanrwst, but seem to have made no actual contact with the rebel forces at any point. But then Glyn Dwr's great ally, the Welsh climate, came to his aid. Contemporary accounts stressed just how horrendous conditions were that autumn. All three of the English expeditions were lashed by torrential rain. Men, horses and supply wagons were swept away as they attempted to ford streams and rivers swollen into raging torrents by the ceaseless rain. Men succumbed to the effects of cold and exposure. To the pouring rain were added gales. King Henry himself narrowly escaped death when his tent collapsed in high winds, and its main pole struck him across the chest. He was only saved by the armour he was wearing at the time.

By 22 September, the bedraggled and beaten English armies were back at their starting points. The king's great expedition had been a total failure. John Hardynge, a squire to Hotspur, is scathing about King Henry's expeditions to Wales:

> The King Henry thrice to Wales went
> In the haytime and the harvest, divers years
> In every time were mists and tempests sent
> Of weather foul that he had never power
> Glendower to know, but o'er his carriage clear
> Owen had at certain straits and passages
> And to our hosts did full great damage
> The king had never but tempest foul and rain
> As long as he was aye in Wales' ground
> Rocks and mists, winds and storms certain
> All men trowed that witches made that stound
> The commons, all of them on England's ground,
> Cursed his going to Wales every year
> For hay and corn were lost both in fire.

Background

Back in London, still smarting from his reverses, Henry received word of a great military triumph by the Percys in the north.

From the start of the year, England's enemies in Scotland had been eyeing the opportunities presented by Henry's setbacks in Wales. From the spring onwards, reports had emanated from Scotland that King Richard was there, alive and well, and that a Scottish invasion of England would be launched in his support. There was indeed an individual in Scotland with a strong physical resemblance to the former king, although the person concerned apparently denied he was Richard and was kept carefully out of sight. Henry believed him to be an Englishman named Thomas Ward of Trumpington. But, imposter though the man might be, reports of Richard's existence caused a great deal of excitement among the former king's English supporters. From the spring of 1402, the pace of their plotting increased. Once again, many were Franciscan friars. One of those apprehended was brought before Henry, who asked him what he would do if Richard were to appear in person: 'I would fight for him, though I had nothing but a stick in my hand!' the prisoner replied defiantly. The shaken king exclaimed: 'You are not my friend and by my head, your head shall fall!' The summer saw more reports of supernatural portents – one of which claimed a sighting of the Devil, apparently dressed as a Franciscan!

Homildon Hill

On the Scottish border at the start of 1402 an uneasy and fragile calm still reigned. Indeed, while Hotspur had been absent in Wales, his father had patched up a temporary truce with the Scots. But the problem remained that, with the confused political situation in Scotland and rival magnates jockeying for power, any such agreement could be broken at any time.

The Scottish 'peace party', headed by the Duke of Rothesay, had hoped to convert the temporary truce into a more permanent peace. However, the dominant force on the Scottish side of the border remained the powerful Douglas family, implacably opposed both to peace with England and to reconciliation with the Percy family. The current head of the Douglas family was Archibald, the 4th Earl. Despite a minor success against Hotspur in a skirmish at Cocksburnspath, Douglas

War for the Throne

was generally an unsuccessful commander, whose ill fortune in war earned him the soubriquet of 'Tyneman' ['Tin Man']. Indeed, right up until the date of his death at the Battle of Verneuil in 1424, Douglas lost almost every encounter in which he was engaged. However, few doubted Douglas's personal courage, and his current determination to pursue a warlike policy against England was heightened by the recent defection to King Henry of his chief rival, George Dunbar.

During the spring of 1402 Douglas's position in Scotland was strengthened by the death of the Duke of Rothesay, almost certainly disposed of by Douglas and his current ally, the Duke of Albany.

Following from this, there were an increasing number of Scottish raids into England. These met with some initial success; however, one party of raiders, led by Sir Patrick Hepburn of Hailes, was intercepted by an English force led by Hotspur and George Dunbar, who was apparently acting as Percy's military adviser. In a brief engagement at Nesbitt Moor on 22 June, the Scots were decisively beaten, Hepburn himself among the dead. This minor English victory served only to inflame the situation. There was already a Scottish army, reportedly 12,000 strong, operating near Carlisle, and Douglas was determined to seek recompense for the recent Scottish reverse.

The Scottish army that had been operating in the vicinity of Carlisle was transferred to the East March and began raids deep into Northumberland. Expecting such a move, the Percys had already mustered their own retainers, plus those of their immediate followers. In September, a Scottish army, believed to be between 10,000 and 12,000 strong, launched a major expedition, which penetrated as far as the River Tyne. The objective of the Percys, with Dunbar, was to intercept this invading force before it could regain the safety of Scotland.

George Dunbar was still with Hotspur and it has been suggested that his advice was heeded in the operations that followed.

Douglas had been joined by men from Galloway, Clydesdale and Lothian, and, in an indication of the divisions wracking Scotland, by George Dunbar's brother and a number of his tenants. The Duke of Albany had reinforced Douglas with a force of knights under Murdoch Stewart, Earl of Fife. A number of other members of the Scottish nobility, including the Earls of Moray, Angus and Orkney, were also present, with a contingent of thirty French knights.

Richard II: a maligned ruler, Richard was erratic and untrustworthy; a lover of the Arts who alienated many of his more warlike magnates, but who could also inspire intense personal loyalty among his supporters. Even after death, Richard remained a serious threat to the survival of the Lancastrian dynasty.

ry IV and his wife, Queen Joanna: a young and vigorous man in 1399, Henry was worn down he threats and difficulties he faced throughout his reign and died in 1413, sick and prematurely d.

Prince Henry: this portrait – a copy of a reputedly contemporary painting – is unusual for the period, being in profile. However, it is noticeable that the left side of Henry's face shows no sign of the scar that would have been very prominent from his injury at Shrewsbury.

The motte at Glyndyfrdwy: Glyn Dwr's residence was probably close by. Here, his supporters mustered prior to the start of his rebellion in September 1400.

The Great Seal of Owain Glyn Dwr as Prince of Wales: this is the only known contemporary depiction of Glyn Dwr and was probably taken from life.

rkworth Castle, Northumberland: as well as being a fortress, Warkworth was the Earl of rthumberland's favourite residence.

Alnwick Castle, Northumberland: the main military stronghold of the Percys.

Pilleth: a view looking west towards Bryn Glas, showing the steep slope up which Mortimer's army advanced. The row of poplars is said to mark the site of a grave pit.

Pilleth: St Mary's Church, near which many of the dead were buried.

Eighteenth-century map showing the site of the Battle of Homildon Hill.

View of Homildon Hill: in the foreground is the 'Battle Stone', said to commemorate the battle.

This aerial view of Shrewsbury makes clear how the old town was protected on three sides by the River Severn. The narrow neck of land on the northern side of the town was protected by the tow walls and castle.

View of battlefield: a view looking north from the battlefield park observation mound towards the ridge east of Albright Hussey – probable location of the initial rebel position.

View of battlefield: a view of the battlefield looking northwards towards the ridge west from Battlefield Church.

Church of St Mary Magdalen (Battlefield Church): built on the orders of Henry IV to commemorate the fallen at the Battle of Shrewsbury. It is said that a mass grave lies under or near the church but no trace has yet been found.

Harlech Castle: another of Edward I's great fortresses, Harlech fell to Glyn Dwr in 1404 and was his headquarters for the next four years. It was regained by English forces in February 1409.

The remains of Aberystwyth Castle: besieged several times during the Glyn Dwr revolt, its eventual recapture by the English in 1408 was a major blow to Glyn Dwr.

Woodbury Hill, Worcestershire: in August 1405 the Franco-Welsh army took position here in the deepest penetration into England by Glyn Dwr.

Background

Many of the Scots had been drawn to Douglas's banner from the mixed motives of seeking vengeance on George Dunbar and for the usual attractions of plunder. Douglas had probably entered England by crossing the River Tweed in the vicinity of Coldstream, and after ravaging the countryside as far as Newcastle, was planning to return the same way. The Scottish chronicler, Walter Bower, described the opening moves in his *Scotichronicon*:

> The new Earl of Douglas, who had custody then of the castles of Edinburgh and Dunbar and who was the king's son-in-law, wished to seek revenge upon the English for the slaughter of the Scots at Nesbit [*sic*]. He approached the governor of Scotland, the Duke of Albany, for his help in strengthening his army, because he said it was [only] with the duke's advice that he would be willing to go to England. The duke gave him his eldest son, Sir Murdoch, with an augmented force of knights and brave men. He therefore assembled a large army in the same year to the number of 10,000 fighting men, including the Earls of Angus and Moray as well as the Master of Fife, and entering England they plundered it as far as Newcastle. As they returned, Sir Henry the younger (otherwise Hotspur) with Sir George Dunbar Earl of March and a large army reached Milfield before them. The Master of Fife and the Earl of Douglas climbed to some rising ground called Homildon, where they waited for the arrival of the English. As they stood on the plain facing the Scots, the English were impatient to attack them on Percy's order, but the Earl of March reined Percy, saying that he should not move, but should send archers who could easily penetrate the Scots as targets for their arrows and defeat and capture them.

The Percys and Dunbar will have expected this, and were aware that the Scots army would be slowed down as a result of the large quantities of booty it was bringing back with it.

The Percys mustered their forces at Milfield-on-Till, around 6 miles from Wooler. Here they lay squarely across the Scots' road to Coldstream and home. Douglas's reaction was to take up a defensive position on Homildon (sometimes referred to as 'Humbledon') Hill, a

1,000-foot high outcrop of the Cheviots. A short distance to the north-west is Harehope Hill, of similar height, separated from Homildon Hill by a steep-sided glen. To the north is a plain where the Rivers Till and Glen meet. Much of the valley floor was probably under cultivation, with some boggy ground on the north-eastern part of what would be the battlefield. The higher ground of the two hills was probably rough pasture.

The English force was drawn partly from the border garrisons, with a number of knights and their retainers, mainly archers. Among those present were the Lord of Greystoke, Sir Henry Fitzhugh, Sir Ralph de Yver, the Lieutenant of Roxburgh, and the Constable of Dunstanburgh Castle. The Percys brought with them a number of their own retainers, including Sir Robert Umfraville and John Hardynge, with a contingent of irate Newcastle townsmen, eager to avenge the losses they had suffered in the Scottish raid. Ralph Neville, Earl of Westmoreland, though not present in person, had sent a contingent of troops to reinforce the Percys. Doubts have been expressed as to whether the Earl of Northumberland was present. Most probably he was, though he may have left operational command to Hotspur and Dunbar. The bulk of the English force probably consisted of archers, with a total strength of perhaps 7,000 men in all.

Douglas's army was in a strong defensive position, although their commander must have realized his men were potentially vulnerable to English archery. The English forces took position on the plain below Homildon Hill. Some versions suggest Hotspur wanted to launch an immediate frontal attack up the slope, and had to be dissuaded by Dunbar. This seems unlikely. Although Hotspur might, on occasion, have had a tendency to rashness, he would hardly have committed such obvious military suicide, especially with so few men-at-arms.

Instead, a force of archers (of unknown numbers) was detached and probably sent up Harehope Hill to open fire on the Scots, with the aim of damaging them sufficiently to force them out of their strong position and on to the attack. There are some doubts regarding the exact location of the English archers, as the contemporary account by Walsingham suggests they were deployed in the dale: that is the ravine between the two hills, and somewhat closer to the Scottish position. In this scenario, the remainder of the English force would have been

Background

deployed on Harehope Hill. Thomas Walsingham, in his *Historia Anglicana*, tells the story from the English viewpoint:

> At that time the Scots, made restless by their usual arrogance, entered England in hostile fashion; for they thought that all the northern lords had been kept in Wales by the royal command; but the Earl of Northumberland the lord Henry Percy, and Henry his son, and the Earl of Dunbar who had lately left the Scots and sworn fealty to the King of England, with an armed band and a force of archers, suddenly flung themselves across the path of the Scots who, after burning and plundering, wanted to return to their own country, so the Scots had no choice but to stop and choose a place of battle. They chose therefore a hill near the town of Wooler, called Homildon Hill, where they assembled with their men-at-arms and archers. When our men saw this, they left the road in which they had opposed the Scots and climbed a hill facing the Scots. Without delay, our archers, drawn up in the dale, shot arrows at the Scottish schiltron, to provoke them to come down. In reply the Scottish archers directed all their fire at our archers, but they felt the weight of our arrows, which fell like a storm of rain, and so they fled.

Walter Bower describes the later stages of the battle in Scottish eyes:

> [Sir John Swinton] shouted out in a harsh voice as if he were a crier, saying, 'Illustrious comrades! Who has bewitched you today that you do not behave in your usual worthy manner? Why do you not join in with their flying arrows as if you were little fallow deer or young mules in pens? Those who are willing should go down with me and we shall move among our enemies in the Lord's name, either to save our lives in so doing or at least to fall as knights with honour.'
>
> On hearing this the most famous and valiant Adam de Gordon of that ilk, who, indeed for a long time had cultivated mortal enmity against the said lord of Swinton following the death of stalwart men-at-arms from both sides in various fights, knelt down before him to ask pardon from him in particular (as the

most worthy knight in arms in the whole of Britain, as he claimed) so that he might be girded as a knight by the hands of the same Sir John. This was done, and a band of a hundred respected knights followed these leaders who had thus been reconciled. They contended intrepidly with a thousand Englishmen; and that whole Scottish group fell dead, though not without a great slaughter of English. It was assuredly believed and it was sworn on oath by some Englishmen, as I have heard, that if the other Scots who had stood on Homildon Hill had fallen on them with like vigour, either the English would have fled, or the Scots would have achieved victory over them.

The dense ranks of the Scottish schiltrons made easy targets for the English bowmen, whose arrows reportedly 'fell like a storm of rain'. In response, the Scottish archers attempted a counter-barrage, but were outshot, in some cases taking flight through the massed troops behind them, causing confusion and gaps in their ranks. According to Walsingham:

> The English bowmen, advancing towards the Scots, smothered them with arrows and made them bristly like a hedgehog, transfixing the hands and arms of the Scots to their own lances. By means of this very harsh rain of arrows they made some duck, they wounded others, and killed many.

This is an excellent description of the disruption and confusion, rather than serious casualties, which the 'arrow storm' was intended to inflict. It also led, probably within a few minutes, to the other desired Scottish reaction. While many of the poorly protected foot soldiers seem to have attempted to escape, at least two attacks against the English were made by parties of mounted knights and nobles. One group was led by Archibald Douglas, who, as Walsingham observes, soon ran into trouble:

> [Douglas] seized a lance and rode down the hill with a troop of his horse, trusting too much to his equipment and that of his men,

Background

who had been improving their armour for three years, and strove to rush on the archers. When the archers saw this, they retreated, but still firing, so vigorously, so resolutely, so effectively, that they pierced the armour, perforated the helmets, pitted the swords, split the lances, and pierced all the equipment with ease. The Earl of Douglas was pierced with five wounds, notwithstanding his elaborate armour. The rest of the Scots who had not descended the hill turned tail, and fled from the flight of arrows. But flight did not avail them, for the archers followed them, so that the Scots were forced to give themselves up, for fear of the death-dealing arrows. The Earl of Douglas was captured; many of those who fled were captured, but many were drowned in the river Tweed, so that the waters devoured, it was said, 500 men. In this flight no lord or knight received a blow from the enemy; but God Almighty gave the victory miraculously to the English archers alone, and the magnates and men-at-arms remained idle spectators of the battle.

A second attack, by about 100 mounted Scots, was led by Sir John Swinton, who had played a distinguished role in Hotspur's defeat at Otterburn, fourteen years previously. Taunting his comrades into a headlong charge, Swinton met with no better fortune than Douglas. The Scottish horse were halted in confusion, making easy targets as they attempted to struggle back up the hill to their starting point.

Not a single Scottish man-at-arms seems to have reached the English position. They and their mounts, dead or wounded, were strewn in front of the English position as Hotspur's men began a ruthless pursuit of the fugitives, Thomas Walsingham noting that: 'flight did not avail them, for the archers followed them, so that the Scots were forced to give themselves up, for fear of the death-dealing arrows'.

Large numbers of Scottish foot soldiers were drowned as they attempted to cross the River Till. The Percys were able to count a rich haul in prisoners – chief among them the wounded Archibald Douglas. Also taken were the Earls of Moray, Angus and Orkney, and over 1,000 others, including many knights. English losses were claimed to

Archers in Battle: the 'Arrow Storm'

One of the most popular misconceptions is the name of the archer and his principal weapon. Neither the terms 'long-bowman' or 'longbow' were in contemporary use. Employment of the latter term has led to the erroneous belief that the bow used by English archers in the period of the Hundred Years' War was some revolutionary new weapon. Although some details are obscure, it is clear that the war bow, in basically the same form as employed at Shrewsbury, had been in use in England from at least the Norman Conquest and possibly earlier.

One of the greatest strengths of the bow was the rapidity with which it could be shot. It was claimed that a well-trained archer could loose off as many as twenty shots in the space of a minute, and although such a rate was, in all probability, rarely achieved or indeed desired, ten aimed shots a minute was the expected standard.

This made it possible for archers to mount an extremely heavy barrage. For example, 5,000 archers could discharge 50,000 arrows in the space of a minute, creating the famed 'arrow storm'. Contemporary writers give an idea of the terrifying impression this had. At Crécy (1346), it was said that the English archers 'stepped forth one pace and let fly their arrows so wholly together and so thick and fast it seemed like snow'. At Edward III's victory over the Scots at Halidon Hill (1331) arrows were 'as thick as motes on the sunbeam'.

In estimating the likely duration of such a barrage, it is worth looking at the supply of arrows generally available to an individual archer.

Most bowmen seem to have started a battle with an immediate supply of two 'sheaves', totalling forty-eight arrows, with perhaps a further one or two dozen arrows carried in their belts for speedy access. In combat, all of these would normally be stuck in front of the archer, point down in the ground. In a continuous barrage, such a supply could be shot off in five or six minutes, after which the archer would have to rely on any additional supplies brought up from the baggage train by the servant, often employed by groups of two or three archers.

Background

> In reality most barrages did not continue long enough for an archer to exhaust his ready supply of arrows. Unless, as may have occurred at Shrewsbury, archers were attempting to provoke an enemy attack, they generally did not begin to shoot until the enemy advance had actually begun. Assuming he did not break in flight, an attacker would instinctively quicken his pace in order to minimize time under enemy fire, which would, in any case, generally only commence when the attacker was within 300 yards of the archers' position. If a dismounted attacking force took as long as three minutes to cover this distance, an archer was unlikely to have discharged more than around thirty arrows.

total no more than five dead. The Percys had won a major victory but one that was to have far-reaching and fatal consequences.

When news of the victory reached King Henry, his immediate reaction was to order that none of the notable Scottish prisoners should be ransomed without his permission and that all should be brought to him at Westminster 'for urgent causes now moving the king'. This did not, as sometimes suggested, represent a distrust of the Percys, but rather the desperate financial position in which the king now found himself. Any ransom paid for the Scots, was, he felt, much more urgently required by the government than by the Percys. Furthermore, Henry was perfectly within his rights according to the accepted rules of war, where it was stated:

And if any man take any prisoner, at once as he is taken in the host that he bring his prisoner to his captain of muster, and that upon pain of losing his part to his said captain or marshal who shall bring him within eight days to the king, constable or marshal, as soon as he goodly may, upon pain to lose his part of him to be given to him that shall give to the constable and marshal first warning thereof.

We do not know how the Percys reacted to these orders, although, given their existing discontent regarding their financial treatment

War for the Throne

by Henry, they can hardly have been happy. However, the Earl of Northumberland himself was apparently willing to obey Henry's instructions. Hotspur was not.

On 20 October the Earl of Northumberland came before the king at Westminster, bringing with him Murdoch, Earl of Fife, Lord Montgomery, Sir William Graham and Sir Adam Forster, with three French knights. Very obvious by their absence were the Earl of Douglas and Hotspur. The prisoners were received sternly but graciously by King Henry, and invited to dine at his table. But before eating the king evidently had a much less digestible encounter with the Earl of Northumberland. The disagreement probably began regarding the absence of the Earl of Douglas, but the argument soon turned to the Percys' financial grievances. The earl apparently reminded the king that payment was still awaited for their services in Wales and on the Scottish border: 'My son and I have spent our all in your service,' he stated with some exaggeration. Henry's response was uncompromising: 'I have no money, and money you shall not have.' To which Northumberland retorted angrily:

> When you entered the kingdom you promised to rule according to your council; you have year by year received large sums from the country, and yet you say that you have nothing, and pay nothing, which angers your commons. God grant you better counsel!

It was probably Hotspur's failure to produce Douglas that had triggered the king's ill-temper. It may be that the earl pleaded Douglas's wounds as the reason for his non-arrival, but the king suspected – rightly – that other factors were involved.

At some point that autumn, Henry is said to have had a personal encounter with Hotspur. Once again, he demanded where Douglas was, and Hotspur retorted that Sir Edmund Mortimer should be allowed to ransom himself. The king refused, saying that he would not allow Glyn Dwr to finance his rebellion by these means. Hotspur was evidently furious: 'Shall a man expose himself to danger for your sake, and you refuse to help him in his captivity?' Henry may have been more aware of what was happening in Wales than Hotspur was,

Background

Surgery

As evidenced by traces of older wounds found on the bodies discovered at Towton, men often recovered from quite serious wounds suffered in battle. Provided no major organ had been damaged, a flesh wound could be sewn up by a surgeon and would heal provided it did not become infected. Infection, resulting in complications such as gangrene, was both widespread and imperfectly understood. Weapons were frequently dirty, particularly arrowheads that had usually been planted in the ground prior to being shot. The main problem, following a major engagement such as Shrewsbury, was that the small numbers of professional surgeons who were available were overwhelmed by the number of casualties requiring treatment. 'Common' soldiers would often have to depend on rough-and-ready 'first aid' from their comrades.

The more prominent casualties, of course, received much speedier attention and in consequence had a better prospect of recovery. The best known of the Shrewsbury casualties was Prince Henry (the future King Henry V). The arrow, most probably with a bodkin-type head, which pierced his face, entered from the left and penetrated his cheekbone as far as the bone behind his nose. It was certainly sufficiently incapacitating that, despite the claims of pro-Lancastrian commentators, he is unlikely to have played any further part in the battle. Dealing with the injury presented the royal physicians with a major problem. For five days the prince was sedated with herb and plant extracts while the king's surgeon, John Bradmore, who had a notable reputation, designed and had made the instrument with which he would attempt to extract the arrowhead. The head of the instrument was inserted into the wound and into the socket of the arrowhead, and a screw mechanism gradually tightened, slowly withdrawing the arrowhead from Henry's face. The prince would have been left with a major scar for the rest of his life, regarded probably as a 'badge' of honour. Most of the common soldiers who received similar wounds almost certainly died excruciating deaths.

and retorted that Mortimer had deliberately led his army into a trap at Pilleth and was a traitor. 'And you are a traitor!' he added, no doubt in reference to Hotspur's retention of the Earl of Douglas and his

War for the Throne

failure to capture Glyn Dwr in the course of their negotiations in the previous year. Indeed, one account suggests that the king went so far as to strike Hotspur in the face and begin to draw his dagger. Hotspur replied: 'by my faith, this shall be the dearest-bought buffet that ever was in England. Not here, but in the Field!'

As Hotspur stormed back to the north of England, Henry received proof of his suspicions regarding Mortimer. Whatever may have been the case at Pilleth, where there was in fact no reason to suspect Sir Edmund of disloyalty, the months of captivity, waiting in vain for assistance from the king, had changed his mind. At some point that autumn he married Glyn Dwr's daughter, Katerin, and on 13 December the alliance with Glyn Dwr was formalized when Sir Edmund wrote to the Mortimer tenants from Owain's quarters at Machynlleth:

To Sir John Grendor, Howell Vaughan and all the gentles and commons of Radnor and Presteigne.

I greet you much and make known to you that Oweyn Glyndwr has raised a war of which the object is, if King Richard be alive, to restore him to his crown, and if not that, my honoured nephew, who is the right heir to the said crown shall be king of England, and seeing that the said Oweyn will assert his right in Wales. And I, seeing and considering that the said quarrel is good and reasonable, have consented to join in it, and to aid and maintain it, and by the grace of God to a good end, amen. I ardently hope and from my heart that you will support and enable me to bring this struggle of mine to a successful issue.

The clouds of rebellion were thickening fast.

Campaign
Chronicle

---◦◦(◦)◦◦---

The Roots of Rebellion

By the winter of 1402 the apparently amicable relationship between King Henry and the Percys was breaking down. It does not necessarily follow that the latter were yet set on the course of rebellion, but dissatisfaction with the monarch they had played such a major part in installing on the throne was clearly growing. One factor to consider when attempting to discover at what point the Percys decided to stake their all on overthrowing Henry is the resources available to them. With the bulk of their estates closely grouped in the north of England, the Percys could, in the short-term, muster greater strength more quickly than could other English magnates or even the king. This should have meant that, in the event of a Percy insurrection, they would initially have overwhelming military strength available. But when they eventually rebelled in 1403 this would not be the case – suggesting they had not been planning open rebellion for any considerable time.

It may have been early in 1403 that Percy contacts were renewed with Owain Glyn Dwr and with Sir Edmund Mortimer, but this time on a much more secretive basis. The go-between may have been John Morys, a Denbigh man who was a confidential servant to Thomas Percy, Earl of Worcester, and who was certainly with Glyn Dwr in the following October. If so, this is the first clear indication that

War for the Throne

Worcester had turned against the new regime. Indeed, Worcester would be regarded by some contemporaries as being 'the instigator of all the troubles'.

On Henry's accession, Thomas Percy had been confirmed as Earl of Worcester and Admiral of England, with the handsome annual annuity of 700 marks. He had continued to be an active member of the King's Council and a leading diplomat. He also had considerable power and influence in South Wales. So why, if the Percys had not been provoked into action by the undoubted rebuffs they had suffered at the end of 1402, did they actually rebel more than six months later?

By 1402 Henry's policy of appointing personal retainers rather than men of national standing to important governmental positions was beginning to cause considerable discontent among the traditional ruling magnates. Thomas Percy was replaced as Steward of the Household, while the Percys' main northern rival, Richard Neville, was created Earl of Westmoreland.

Westmoreland's powers were steadily expanded in the following months. He replaced Hotspur as Keeper of Roxburgh. More significantly one of his supporters replaced Thomas Percy as Steward.

In the opening months of 1403, the rivalry between the Percys and Ralph Neville was deepening. There had been disputes regarding payment for those of Neville's retainers who had fought at Homildon Hill, and there had been clashes regarding the prisoners still held by the Percys. Henry, however, still appears to have had no suspicion of serious Percy disaffection. In March 1403 he presented the earl and his son with what, from one aspect, appeared a generous offer, but which would in reality turn out to be a poisoned chalice.

The Scottish defeat at Homildon Hill seemed to have opened the opportunity for an English counterstroke, and on 2 March the king informed the Percys that the whole of the Douglas lands in Southern Scotland, as far as, and including, Galloway, were theirs – provided, of course, that they could conquer them. It appeared – in the short term at least – that Henry had come down in favour of the Percys over the House of Neville. In fact, rather than a favour, his action may have been intended as a device to keep his restive Northern allies occupied.

In Wales, too, operations were under way. On 3 March Prince Henry, at the age of 16 regarded as ready to assume a command in the field, was appointed the king's deputy in Wales, with powers to summon the levies of the border counties. More immediately, however, a force of 1,100 men-at-arms and 3,800 archers was mustered at Chester. These were, apparently, professional soldiers and Henry was joined by Thomas Percy, Earl of Worcester, in the role of adviser and mentor. Glyn Dwr himself was reported to be active in the Hope area, only a few miles from Chester.

It was not until May that Prince Henry, clearly eager to prove his ability in the field, began his campaigning. Early in May he rode south-west out of Chester, in a raid designed to sting Glyn Dwr himself.

On 15 May, back in Shrewsbury, the Prince reported his success to his father:

> We have among other matters been lately informed that Owen de Glyndowdry [*sic*] has assembled his forces and those of other rebels adhering to him in great numbers; purposing to commit inroads and in case any resistance be made to him by the English, to come to battle with them, or so he vaunted to his people.
>
> Wherefore we took our force and marched to a place of the said Oweyn [*sic*], well built, which was his principal mansion, called Sycarth, where we thought we should have found him if he had any inclination to fight in the manner he had said, but on our arrival there we found nobody; and therefore caused the whole place to be burned and several other houses near it belonging to his tenants. We then marched straight to his other place of Glendowery to seek for him there and we caused a fine lodge in his park to be destroyed by fire and laid waste all the country around. We there halted for the night and certain of our people sallied forth into the country and took a gentleman of the neighbourhood who was one of the said Oweyn's chief captains. This person offered five hundred pounds for his ransom to preserve his life and to be allowed two weeks for the raising of this sum; but this offer was not accepted and he received death, as did several of his companions who were taken the same day.
>
> We then proceeded to the commote of Ederynion in Merionethshire and there laid waste a fine and populous country; thence we went to Powys, and there being want of provender in Wales for

horses we made our people carry oats with them and pursued our march.

This raid, while demonstrating Prince Henry's ruthless approach to war – he would later in his career comment that 'War without fire is like sausages without mustard' – had been largely symbolic. Glyn Dwr was now playing for much higher stakes than the restoration of his original estates, which he was probably surprised had been spared for so long.

Stationed now in Shrewsbury, Prince Henry soon faced problems. A fortnight after his raid, he was writing to the king:

> our soldiers desire to know if they will be paid for the third month of the present quarter and tell us that they will not wait here, unless they are soon paid their wages according to their indentures. We pray you very dearly that you will order our payment for the said month or otherwise let us know and take order promptly for the safety of these marches. For the rebels hear every day if we are paid, and they know well without payment we cannot continue and they strive to raise all the forces of North Wales and South Wales to over-ride and destroy the march and the counties adjoining thereto; and there is no resistance here, so that they can well accomplish their malice; and when our men shall have retreated from us, it is necessary that we should by all means retreat into England, there to be disgraced forever.
>
> At present we have very great expenses, and have made all the pawning we may of our little jewels to defray them, for too our castles of Aberystwyth and Harlech are besieged and have been for a long time and we must rescue and provision them within ten days and besides defend the March around us with our third body against the entry of the rebels.

It would appear that the two castles were, for the moment, saved either by the despatch of heavily escorted supplies overland, or by sea.

But Glyn Dwr was actively preparing what would be a major summer campaign. In June he was reported to be once again active in the Radnor area, while King Henry ordered the levies of Shropshire,

Campaign Chronicle

Worcester, Gloucester and Hereford to be ready to take the field against the Welsh. But once again he was effectively crippled by lack of funds.

Meanwhile, pressure on the king from the Percys was mounting. In May the Earl of Northumberland wrote to the king's council to point out that the Scots had until 1 August to relieve Ormiston Castle, and that he lacked the money to field a force to meet them. On the other hand, although the Percys made complaints regarding the alleged lack of financial assistance from the king, they must have been well-informed of the parlous state of royal finances. The letter sent by Northumberland on 24 May to the royal council asked for the payment of £20,000 by 24 June. It was not a particularly aggressive communication, and it seems that the intent was to use the money to hire more English troops to oppose the Scots. At the same time pleas for support were sent to a large number of English magnates. It may well have been the replies to these that the Percy chronicler, John Hardynge, later claimed to have seen at Warkworth Castle, and which he wrongly interpreted as being promises to support a Percy uprising against King Henry.

The Percy aim was to achieve complete political and territorial domination of the north of England, together with full command of the Scottish border. In this latter aim they had suffered a reverse when Hotspur lost control of Roxburgh to the Nevilles. They were also certainly angered by the king's rejection of their proposed conciliatory approach to Glyn Dwr. Apart from plunging the crown into the expense of prolonged conflict in Wales, this also drew off troops the Percys hoped would reinforce them on the Scottish border. Both this and Henry's refusal to ransom Mortimer demonstrated that he was acting increasingly independently from the Percys, who almost certainly had thought – when they in effect installed Henry – that at least so far as their own dynastic interests were concerned, he would prove a reliable instrument.

On the other hand, with mounting difficulties facing him on all sides, the king had every reason to remain on good terms with the Percys, and to keep them occupied in order to lessen the possibility of their interfering in matters outside their own immediate concerns. It was probably for these reasons that, on 2 March, the Percys were

War for the Throne

granted all the lands belonging to the Earl of Douglas. In theory this committed the English crown to supporting the Percys' claims in Scotland, as well as their right to act independently in enterprises aimed at their own aggrandizement. Incidentally, and tacitly, by this action Henry also abandoned his demand that Douglas be handed over to him. And if the Percys succeeded in making their award good, then the Nevilles would be totally eclipsed, and George Dunbar, Scottish Earl of March, left with a reduced amount of territory islanded in Percy land. In fact, the king seemed to have given in totally to Percy demands.

The Percys must have realized the problems that came with Henry's 'grant', but neither were they willing to pass up such an opportunity to extend their power and influence in the north compared with that of the Nevilles. So, as soon as the campaigning season opened, Hotspur, with the Percy levies of Northumberland, and accompanied by George Dunbar, Earl of March, advanced north. Dunbar evidently hoped to recover his own lands, but the first target of the invaders was a small fortress known as the Tower of Cocklaw, whose owner declined to surrender.

It appears that Hotspur and Dunbar were ill-prepared for siege warfare, for they made little impression on the defiant Scottish garrison. A six-week truce was agreed. If by the end of August, they had not been relieved, the garrison of Cocklaw would surrender.

It appears that the Percys were hoping in this way to force the Scots to put an army in the field, against which they might repeat their success at Homildon Hill. In the meantime their financial difficulties grew steadily more acute.

It has been claimed that Cocklaw was not put under serious siege, and the Percys' action was designed to force the Scots into a 'truce', either to release the Percys' own forces or as a prelude to obtaining active Scottish support in their intrigues against King Henry. There has also been some confusion regarding the location of Cocklaw, with Ormiston sometimes regarded as a separate place. In fact, Cocklaw Castle was situated just outside the village of Ormiston, about 4 miles to the east of Hawick. Far from being a minor outpost just inside Scotland, Cocklaw was in fact a critical garrison, in the heart of Douglas territory.

Campaign Chronicle

The Percys, accompanied by George Dunbar, emphasized the seriousness of their efforts by raiding deep into Teviotdale. In short, although the Percys were almost certainly still in touch with both Glyn Dwr and Mortimer, at this stage they probably had no immediate intention of rebelling.

Henry evidently did not, or could not, respond to a plea for assistance that Northumberland now made, taking the view that the Percys should be able to rely on their own resources, which ought to be sufficient to take Cocklaw, and on 26 June the earl wrote again, from Haughhead in North Yorkshire. This time his tone was stronger. He accused the king of failing to support the Percys or give them appropriate payments. Henry had in fact sent them sufficient money to maintain the border defences, but insufficient to invade Scotland and it was clear that he could not, or would not, place any additional funding at their disposal. Money was urgently required, and for the first time, particularly in the signature of 'your Matthias', there was the implication that those who had made and unmade kings previously might do so again.

It must have been within the next few days that the decision to rebel was taken. The Percys were, in fact, at a serious disadvantage in striking at this time. Most of their northern forces were tied down in Scotland or on the border, and could not be removed without the risk of the Scots taking advantage of their absence.

By now it seems clear that Thomas Percy, Earl of Worcester, still currently with Prince Henry at Shrewsbury, was actively committed to the family cause. Indeed it was claimed by some that he was the prime mover in the insurrection. Certainly he seems to have been the most intelligent of the family, and was in touch with events at Court. He was also in an excellent position to secure or neutralize Prince Henry. He will also have been able to make his family aware of the considerable discontent among the professional soldiers at Shrewsbury. This may initially have been because of lack of pay, but it is reasonable to assume there were a number of Richard's old Cheshire Guard among them, whose loyalties still lay with their former master, and whom someone of Worcester's persuasive powers would find easy to suborn. It may have been because of this that Hotspur, almost certainly with his father's knowledge and approval (despite the earl's later denials),

War for the Throne

decided to raise his standard in Cheshire. This strategy was not without considerable risk. Although Cheshire was a hotbed of pro-Ricardian sympathies, Hotspur's own record there was not one certain to bring him support now. He had, after all, been actively involved in Richard's overthrow, and had also been responsible for the suppression of the Cheshire Rising of 1400.

But the deciding factor was probably Cheshire's military potential. For over a century, the men of Cheshire had been renowned both for their military skill and their experience as soldiers. Cheshire men had played a major role in the Welsh wars of King Edward I, and during the Hundred Years' War had been a mainstay of Edward III's and the Black Prince's armies. Cheshire troops had seen action at Crécy, Poitiers and Najera, and Cheshire soldiers – such as Sir Hugh Calverley – had gained an international reputation and made personal fortunes in the course of the French wars, and in the notorious mercenary 'Free Companies', which sprang up afterwards.

Many Cheshire men saw service in the contingents raised to serve in France. In 1338 Cheshire contributed 350 mounted archers; eight years later it was ordered that 1,500 men be raised in Cheshire to follow the Earl of Lancaster in Aquitaine. In 1356 the Black Prince demanded 500 mounted archers. It may be that this number proved too large to produce, although certainly 300 were provided. Most of the commanders of the contingents serving in France were the landless younger sons of minor gentry, who raised by indenture the men who followed them. They often returned home to Cheshire to recruit, frequently from their own locality. In 1355 Sir Ralph Mobberley's contingent consisted of knight, esquire and around thirty-two mounted archers. Most of these were recruited within a 10-mile radius centred on Mobberley's estates. Many of them were already followers of Mobberley, with an inner core recruited from relatives, tenants and neighbours. In some cases the more prominent of these would bring their own retainers. There was also a tradition of some English garrisons in France being associated with Cheshire troops. This was especially the case in Guyenne in the 1370s and 1380s. By the closing decades of the fourteenth century there was a significant pattern of professional military service in Cheshire. In 1392, John Massey of Puddington contracted to raise ten men-at-arms and forty archers for

Campaign Chronicle

service in Ireland, though many others contracted for fewer – in some cases just for a single archer. Service in the French wars led to close bonds between many Cheshire men, either from existing kinship or the relationship known as 'brothers in arms' – a recognized bond that carried with it obligations of support. This seems to have been quite common among Cheshire troops, who would continue to serve together under different employers of various nationalities.

Considering the key roles given by King Richard to Cheshire men, it was something of a surprise when, in 1399, the pro-Ricardian faction in the county apparently folded without resistance. This was partly because many of those who might have sided with Richard were still absent in Ireland, and because of lack of effective leadership by the king himself.

Even so, an attempt was made to rescue Richard on his journey to London, and in 1400 the leaders of the Epiphany Revolt called on the men of Cheshire for assistance. On 22 May, King Henry issued a general pardon to the Cheshire men, with around 125 exceptions. Among these were forty-one members of Richard's Guard, including John Legh, John Donne, Thomas Beeston and Thomas Holford, with a number of citizens of Chester, where there had been two unsuccessful attempts to secure the city for the rebels.

News of the failure of the rebellion caused the Cheshire men to disperse. Hotspur was put in charge of extinguishing the embers of revolt when he was appointed Justicar of Chester, with most key posts given to outsiders from the county. In a further sign of royal disfavour, inhabitants of Cheshire were forbidden to seek legal redress for any damage allegedly committed by Henry's supporters in 1399.

There seems to have been continuing unrest and lawlessness in the principality, though this may have been limited by raising forces there for Henry's campaign in Scotland. Sir John Massey of Puddington was ordered to muster sixty men-at-arms and 500 archers. Significantly, five of the watch commanders of Richard's Guard were involved in recruiting, only one of them, Richard Cholmondeley, not having been implicated in the 1400 rising.

However, the outbreak of Glyn Dwr's rising placed an increasing strain on Cheshire. As well as the financial burden, a number of leading Cheshire gentry were called away to serve in the English garrisons in

War for the Throne

Wales or elsewhere, while Thomas Percy, Earl of Worcester, recruited a large number of Cheshire men to serve with him under Prince Henry. This left something of a leadership vacuum in the county, which Hotspur, as Justicar, was able to fill.

The direct impact of the war on Cheshire itself was fairly limited – trade with the Welsh, even if officially forbidden, seems to have continued unabated, while military activity was largely confined to the area west of the River Dee. The greater impact was on the manpower of the county, with regular demands for troops to serve in Wales.

Hotspur may be presumed to have retained some links with the Cheshire leadership after 1402, although this did not apparently extend to any detailed planning for rebellion.

His plan to rely on forces raised in the principality to spearhead the Percy rebellion was something of a gamble, however. His own record there had been somewhat mixed, both in terms of military success and in his relationship with the local population. But the uncertainties were outweighed both by the potential advantages and because Hotspur possessed few other practicable alternatives. A rising in Cheshire was likely to come as a complete surprise to the king. It would also be taking place in the part of England with the greatest amount of experienced military manpower available.

Hotspur apparently slipped away from Cocklaw in early July with a handful of companions. Somewhat surprisingly, his prisoner, Archibald Earl of Douglas, with around twenty Scottish knights, was among them. At first sight this is puzzling. It may be that Hotspur had promised Douglas restoration of an enlarged share of Southern Scotland in the event of victory, and a chance to strike at his hated rival, George, Earl of March. It is equally possible that Douglas joined Hotspur in a spirit of military adventure.

Hotspur rode south through Yorkshire, where he certainly must have consulted with his father. Northumberland himself would claim later that he had played no part in the rebellion, but this seems highly unlikely. What does seem clear is that a letter was received at this point from King Henry, announcing his intention of marching north in person to assist the Percys. This clearly came as bad news to Northumberland, who, in contradiction to his previous pleas, wrote back to Henry that such assistance was not required. The Percys probably suspected that

Campaign Chronicle

Henry had got wind of their plans. This indeed is possible: when, on 10 July, from Higham Ferrars in Northamptonshire, the king wrote to the royal council announcing his intention of marching north to 'give aid and comfort to our very dear and loyal cousins the Earl of Northumberland and his son Henry in the fight honourably undertaken between them and the Scots', he added in a postscript that the council should take heed of some additional information that would be given to them verbally by the king's messenger, Elmyn Leget. It is open to question that this information may have included suspicions regarding the Percys' loyalty.

On 12 July Henry reached Nottingham, where he received the first reports of Hotspur's arrival at Chester, and his raising of the standard of revolt. The younger Percy had arrived in Chester with 160 followers, including a few recruited in Lancashire on 9 July. Staying in the house of one Petronella Clarke, he immediately began to call out the men of Cheshire in rebellion against King Henry.

By this time Glyn Dwr's summer campaign was in full swing. He began operations with a spirited attack on 1 July against Brecon Castle, which was repulsed, but the result was widespread alarm among the English-held garrisons of mid and South Wales. The rebels were obviously out in strength and the whole position of the English forces seemed imperilled.

Glyn Dwr had with him two of his leading commanders, Rhys Gethin and Rhys Ddu, suggesting that the Welsh were operating in at least three large bodies. The Welsh forces pressed south-westwards into the valley of the River Towey, an area hitherto untouched by the rebellion, but whose inhabitants now flocked to join Glyn Dwr.

News of defeat was sent to John Faireford, a royal official at Brecon, by Jenkin Hanard, Constable of Dynevor Castle:

Dear Friend,

Owain Glyn Dwr, Henry Don, Rhys Ddu, Rhys Griffiths ap Llewellyn, Rhys Gethin, have won the town of Carmarthen and Wigmor, Constable of the Castle, has yielded up the castle to Oweyn [sic], who has burned the town and slain of men of the town more than fifty and they are and that is a great peril for me and all that are here with me, for they have made a vow that they will kill us all, therefore I pray you that you will not boggle [scare] us but send us a warning within a short time whether we shall have any help or not; or if there be no help coming that we may steal away by night to Brecon ...

Written in haste and dread, Faireford urged the king's officers in Hereford to act:

Rees ap Griffith, of the county of Carmarthen, William ap Philip, Henry Don and his son with many of their adherents were on Monday last treasonably rising in the plain country, against the king our most sovereign Lord and hath laid siege to the Castle of Dynevor with a great force of rebels. And moreover it was certified to me by Ralph Monnington and others who were in the castle of Llandovery how that Owain Glyn Dwr and his false troops were at Llandovery on Tuesday and that the men there being surprised they in the said castle are assured and secured to him, and three hundred of the rebels were at their ease, lying round in siege of the said castle and at night were lodged in Llandeilo, at which time the men of the said county and of other Lordships around were also assured and sworn to him. And at this same Wednesday the same Owain, and all other rebels are on their march towards this town of Brecon for the destruction of the town, which God avert, and after they purpose to make a diversion against other parties in the March if they be not resisted [...]

And you will know that all the Welsh nation being taken a little by surprise is adhering to this evil purpose of rebellion and they are assured thereunto, how fully, from one day to another by the support they give to it, clearly appears more openly; and I pray you, please to ordain the most speedy resistance against the rebels that you can and if any mounted expedition be made, be pleased to do this first in these Lordships of Brecon and Cantref Sellyf.

Written at Brecon this Wednesday afternoon and in great haste.

Campaign Chronicle

On 6 July, Glyn Dwr, with an army precisely numerated at 8,420 spearmen, captured Carmarthen, though he was quickly forced to abandon it after a series of minor reverses. The Welsh were meeting with their usual problem of capturing the English-held castles, without which, though they might dominate the surrounding countryside, they could seldom gain uncontested control of an area.

Sir John Skidmore was Constable of Careg Cennan Castle, and would later mark a shift in his allegiance by marrying Glyn Dwr's daughter.

For the moment, he remained loyal to the English regime, and wrote:

> For as much as I say I may not spare any man from this place away from me to certify neither my king nor the lord my province in the mischief of the countryside about, nor no man pass by anyway, hence I pray and require you that you certify them how all Carmarthenshire, Kidwelly, Carnwaltham and Isckenyed were sworn to Owain yesterday. And he lay tonight in the castle of Dryslwyn with Rhys ap Griffeth and there I was on truce and prayed for a safe conduct under his seal to send home my wife and her mother and her train but he would not grant me. This day he is about Carmarthen and thinks to abide there until he may have town and castle; and his purpose then is to go into Pembrokeshire, for he holds all the castles and towns in Kidwelly, Gowersland and Glamorgan for the same countries have undertaken the siege of them until they be won.
>
> Excite the king's advisers that they should excite the king here in all haste to avenge himself on some of his false traitors he has cherished overmuch and to rescue the towns and castles in these countries, for I dread full sore there be few true to maintain them.

Faireford did indeed write urgently to King Henry:

> Ordain a remedy for the resistance and destruction of the traitors which are daily reinforced and from time to time cause great evil and destruction to your faithful subjects without any resistance; considering my most gracious lord that if assistance come not

speedily, all the castles and towns and your loyal subjects within them are in great peril and on the point of being utterly ruined for default of succour and good government.

The sheriffs of Herefordshire pointed out to the king that they could provide little assistance without outside aid, and the Archdeacon of Hereford, Richard Kingeston, followed up their comments with a blunt warning:

> Letters are arriving from Wales containing intelligence by which you may learn that the whole country is lost if you do not go there as quickly as possible. For which reason may it please you to prepare to set out with all the power that you can muster and march day and night for the salvation of these parts. And may it please you to reflect that it will be a great disgrace as well as a loss, to lose or suffer to be lost in the beginning of your reign a country which your noble ancestors have won and for so long a time peaceably possessed. For people talk very unfavourably.

By now, however, the worst of the crisis in South Wales appeared to be over. On 12 July, the townsfolk of Caerleon reported to their counterparts at Monmouth that

> There was this day a battle between the worthy baron of Carew and Owain Glyn Dwr, and we do wish you to know that the night before the battle Owain was on purpose to have avoided him and to find out whether the way was clear to pass, if he had need of it. He sent 700 of his men to search the ways and there they met with the baron's men who slew everybody so there was none on that scene alive.

They also reported a rumour suggesting that Glyn Dwr had been consulting a local soothsayer:

> He sent for Hopkyn ap Thomas of Gower to come and speak with him on truce and Hopkyn came. Owain he prayed him, inasmuch as he held him to be a Master of Brut, that he should

tell him how and in what manner it should fall out for him, and he told him that he would be captured in a short time between Carmarthen and Gower, and the taking would be under a black banner.

It was unfortunate Hopkyn's knowledge did not apparently extend to telling Glyn Dwr of developments to the north.

The Shrewsbury Campaign

Hotspur and his party had entered Chester without resistance, and indeed were apparently greeted with enthusiasm by its leading citizens. Hotspur's first actions were to call the men of Cheshire to arms, and to issue a proclamation calculated to win their support. He promised that within three days they would be joined by King Richard in person and an army under the Earl of Northumberland. This was not a pretence that could for long be maintained, and it may be doubted how many of Richard's former leading supporters actually believed in it. But in the short term, it certainly brought the Cheshiremen, especially the veteran archers of King Richard's Guard, flocking to Hotspur's banner. To one chronicler, whose awe of them is clear from his words, they were: 'mystery men meddlers of wrongs who played with poleaxes and the points of swords'.

Of the 122 known rebels who joined Hotspur, ninety-five came from Cheshire, Shropshire or just across the border into Wales. The rising seems to have begun in the Hundred of Bucklow, possibly because Hotspur entered the county in that area, crossing the River Mersey to the south of Manchester. Bucklow was the home of two of Richard's leading supporters, John Legh of Bowden and Thomas Holford, both watch commanders in the Cheshire Guard. A key figure in bringing out support for Hotspur was Sir John Massey of Tatton. He had served with the Black Prince and John of Gaunt in Spain, and had taken part in Richard's ill-fated expedition to Ireland. Massey had not been involved in the earlier conspiracies following Richard's deposition, and seemed to have come to terms with the new regime, but now took up arms, along with his sons, Thomas and Richard. The ties of kinship and military service were shown as Sir William Leigh of Baguley, a colleague of Massey in the local administration, also joined the rebels. They had served together in Ireland and were certainly among the first to join Hotspur.

Peter Dutton, who had been Constable of Chirk Castle under Richard, and had served in Ireland, also joined. Another committed rebel was Peter Warburton, who, in 1400, had left the army in Wales without permission, and Robert Toft of Toft Hall south of Knutsford, a close associate of Legh and Holford.

John Kynaston of Dunham Massey also had extensive interests in North Wales, and was closely associated with the Glyn Dwr Revolt from its outset. Kynaston was linked with another principal rebel, John Done of Utkington, the Forester of Delamere, who had had contact with Hotspur as early as 1400. In 1403 he raised the tenants of the Lestrange estates at Ellesmere in Shropshire, with the assistance of Richard Deenbourgh, Rector of Llanymynech, an interesting example of the influence local pro-Ricardian clergy had in raising support for the rebellion. Done may have been one of Hotspur's contacts with Glyn Dwr, and certainly was his chief organizer in the border areas of North Shropshire.

The Macclesfield Hundred of Cheshire produced two leading rebels: Sir Robert Legh of Alder and Sir Lawrence Fitton of Gawsworth. Legh had been retained by Richard, and made Constable of Oswestry. Despite the beheading in 1400 of his half-brother, Peter Legh, Sir Robert had appeared reconciled to the new regime. Fitton had served in Richard's ill-fated Irish expedition of 1399. It is unclear what motivated Legh and Fitton to join Hotspur. Both had apparently prospered under the new regime. It may be that with most of their neighbours joining the rebellion, they felt pressured into supporting them. In general, it seems that the degree of recruitment was greatest close to Hotspur's route to Chester, and at this distance of time it is unclear how far threats or other forms of coercion played a part.

In Northwich Hundred there were two prominent supporters of Hotspur, Sir Richard Venables of Kinderton and Sir Richard Vernon of Shipford. The fact that both were later to be executed for their part in the rebellion may suggest they were among its more prominent leaders, or they may simply have been unlucky enough to be made examples of. Both men had been retained by Richard, and had served in Ireland, but there is no evidence of their being opposed to the new regime before the 1403 rebellion. They did, however, have some connections with Robert Bostock, a captain in King Richard's Guard, who may have been the leading recruiter for Hotspur in Northwich Hundred. Another rebel, Sir Thomas Grosvenor of Hulme, was the father-in-law of Sir Richard Vernon.

The pattern of recruitment on the march would continue. When Hotspur eventually marched south into Shropshire via the Eddisbury Hundred of Cheshire, he was joined by two former captains of Richard's Guard, John Done of Utkington and Thomas Beeston. Their influence alone was enough to ensure large numbers of recruits from Eddisbury Hundred, including many of Richard's Guard. Sir Richard Winnington, another Irish veteran, also took up arms, bringing to Hotspur's banner his relatives, John Beeston of Tiverton and John Winnington, who had been a royal archer in 1397. Arthur Davenport of Calverley was another former retainer of Richard, while another, Richard Bromley of Baddington, had raised archers for Henry's Scottish campaign of 1400, and now did the same for Hotspur.

Perhaps surprisingly, there is little evidence of intensive recruiting in the town of Chester itself. The names of only two Chester rebels, Thomas Allen and Robert Goldsmith, are known. Allen seems to have acted as go-between for Hotspur and the Earl of Worcester in the days immediately prior to the rising, and after the rebellion gave surety for the behaviour of John Ambell, Hotspur's chaplain.

In Broxton Hundred, nearly all the known rebels were from the south-eastern corner of the district, which lay directly on Hotspur's line of march. One was Richard Cholmondeley, a former watch commander in Richard's Guard, who had not been involved in the previous plots against the new regime. He brought with him two neighbours, Thomas Huxley and Hugh Bickerton. Another rebel, John Aldersley, had previously served under Thomas Beeston. John Knight of Clutton and Daniel Bickerley had been involved in the 1400 rebellion. The most important rebel in this area was Sir Hugh Browe, a veteran soldier with service in France and Ireland and against the Welsh rebels. His son Robert rose with him.

Recruits also came in from across the Welsh border. John Healey was a former deputy constable of Flint Castle, and Daffydd ap Bletchyn ap Ithel, who only a month previously had been appointed as one of the defenders of the commote of Coleshill against the Welsh rebels. There were also the parsons of Dodleston, Pulford, Hanckley and Hawarden.

Possibly because Hotspur himself didn't recruit there, there were fewer volunteers from the Cheshire Hundred of Wirral. However, they included several prominent local figures, among them Sir William Stanley and Sir John Poole with various relatives and dependants. Both Stanley and Poole had hitherto appeared reconciled to the events of 1399; both had taken part in the Scottish expedition of 1400, and perhaps significantly, may have been with Hotspur at Homildon Hill, for both had Scottish prisoners in their custody. They may also have served with Hotspur in Wales. Poole had been governor of Caernarvon and Beaumaris Castles, and was a leading figure in the English war effort.

It is unclear how far dissatisfaction with the course of the war against Glyn Dwr may have influenced the rebels. Though Cheshire itself had suffered little material damage so far, some of the rebels' trading operations in Wales will undoubtedly have suffered, and there may have been resentment on the edicts against trading with the Welsh, issued by Henry, although these were widely flouted.

Previous military contacts with Hotspur were undoubtedly a major factor. Of the leading rebels, Sir Richard Winnington, Browe, Poole, and Sir William Stanley had all served with him in North Wales, though John Hulgrave, a Ricardian who had also served with Hotspur, chose to remain loyal to the new regime.

Only around 100 named rebels are known for 1403, compared with 139 for 1400. In fact, the rebellion was considerably more widespread in 1403, suggesting that, with the exigencies of the Welsh war in mind, Henry's government chose to overlook many of those who joined Hotspur. Of the known rebels, twenty-five had been retainers of Richard, along with the sons of a number of others. Around a quarter of Richard's known retainers joined Hotspur, which might suggest that the great majority remained quiet. However, figures are too incomplete to be confident of this. In Broxton Hundred, for example, a number of those known to have been in arms in 1400 did not join the 1403 rebellion. It was the case, of course, that rebels who had been pardoned in 1400 had much more to lose by rebelling again. And proximity to Prince Henry and the forces at Shrewsbury may have served to make some cautious. Contributions from some areas, for example Wirral, may have been lessened by the short duration of the campaign.

The summons sent out by Hotspur called for a rendezvous of his supporters at the key road junction of Sandiway on 12 July. We can imagine each of the prominent rebels mustering their retainers and tenants, the more prudent sending a son to lead them rather than taking up arms themselves. Although claims were initially made that King Richard would join the rebel army at Sandiway, this pretence could not be kept up for long, and Hotspur was forced to amend his proclamation to one in support of reform of the government, and a rather lukewarm support for the claim to the throne of the Earl of March.

Hotspur, whose gamble had paid off to the extent of providing him with significant Cheshire support, had now to decide on his next move. His only other followers were the small band who had accompanied him from the north, which included his squires, Thomas Knayton and Roger Salwayn, the keeper of Carlisle Castle gaol, William Felour, a handful of supporters from Lancashire and the Earl of Douglas and his twenty Scottish knights.

At some point, providing significant additional military muscle for his army, Thomas Percy, Earl of Worcester, defected from the force with Prince Henry at Shrewsbury, bringing with him some 200 men-at-arms and 800 archers – almost half the prince's force.

This is a mysterious episode, of which we know tantalizingly little. It may be that Worcester had hoped to bring over the entire Shrewsbury force, discontented as it was because of pay arrears. He may even have hoped to secure Shrewsbury itself and take the prince into custody. If such was the plan, it clearly misfired, and Hotspur had to decide on his next move. Ruled out from the start was any possibility of moving back across the Midlands to link with any forces being raised by his father. Such a march, through areas where little support was to be expected, would also take him squarely onto the path of King Henry, moving north towards the Scottish border. Much more promising was a rapid march south. The initial objective was Shrewsbury. It may have been hoped that the weakened garrison might yet defect, or at least yield or retreat without attempting to hold the town. Possession of Shrewsbury would give Hotspur a recruiting centre adjacent to the presumably sympathetic Mortimer estates of the mid-Wales Marches, and might be expected to provide additional military supplies.

Less clear is whether, as frequently asserted, Hotspur hoped to link with Glyn Dwr. It is unclear how far Hotspur had co-ordinated his plan and strategy with those of the Welsh leader. There had certainly been some contact between them over recent weeks, with William Lloyd and John Kynaston acting as go-betweens. There is, however, no evidence to support Hardynge's claim that Hotspur hoped to join forces with Glyn Dwr on the banks of the Severn.

In early July, as we have seen, Glyn Dwr was operating in south-west Wales. This would still have allowed him time to rendezvous with Hotspur in the vicinity of Shrewsbury if such had been the intention. The available evidence suggests either that the operations of Hotspur and the main Welsh forces were in fact unconnected, or that Glyn Dwr's intention was to occupy and draw off English forces in South Wales and prevent them from reinforcing Prince Henry or the king. And although the Welsh troops were better equipped than sometimes suggested, the results of most of their engagements in open battle with English forces suggests they were poorly prepared to encounter them in a set piece battle.

So there is no clear evidence as to whether Glyn Dwr was expected to join Hotspur in the later stages of the campaign. Certainly it is unlikely that Percy intended to face the king in battle until he had all available troops at his disposal. It is probable that the plan was for the Earl of Northumberland – leaving the original Northern army to guard the Scottish border – to raise the Percy tenants in Yorkshire, with other sympathizers, and then move south. King Henry, it was probably hoped, would either have continued to march north (so making it possible to trap him between the Percys, father and son) or would fall back on London, in the vicinity of which a decisive battle of the campaign could be fought.

King Henry reached Nottingham on the evening of 12 July. It was evidently here that he received what, at this point, was little more than a rumour of Hotspur's revolt. His reaction was to alter the direction of his march, moving westwards and spending the next two days at

Campaign Chronicle

Derby, where he could block any move by Hotspur to march north-east towards his father in Yorkshire. On the 17th, at Lichfield, Henry at last received firm information on events in Cheshire, and sent an urgent message to his council in London:

> the king encloses a letter drafted with the advice of the lords, knights and esquires at present in his company, to be sent to the archbishop of Canterbury, all the prelates and the lords temporal, to tell them of his plans, and let the council not fail in this. Henry Percy has risen against the king, calling him 'Henry of Lancaster'. And has proclaimed that Richard is still alive. The king wants all members of the council wherever they may be to hasten to him, except the treasurer, who is to remain behind and raise all the loans he can.

It is not clear how many troops the king initially had with him, though details of an army he had under his command in April 1405 may provide a rough indication. On that occasion he had a personal retinue of 144 men-at-arms and 720 archers. With him also were the retinues of a number of the nobility. A document in the Exchequer of 17 July lists payments to a force totalling four barons, twenty knights, 476 esquires and 2,500 archers. This probably refers to the expedition against the Welsh of the previous autumn, but is another indication of the likely size of the army that Henry had with him initially. Another reference credits him with 2,500 archers in July 1403.

The sheriffs of the Midland counties were ordered to call out the militia and march to join the king with all haste. There is some indication that Henry initially considered falling back towards London, in order to link with forces coming from that direction. But in the rather small land area of England, an insurrection could quickly grow out of control if unchecked, and the king had now been joined by that experienced soldier, George Dunbar, Earl of March, who had slipped away from the forces besieging Cocklaw, probably on realizing that Hotspur had left. The rebellion gave Dunbar the unrivalled opportunity to place his expertise at the king's disposal, probably with the hope of regaining his estates on the Scottish border as a result of a Percy defeat. He urged Henry to march west and confront Hotspur before the rebellion could spread or the Earl of Northumberland reinforce his son.

Hotspur, meanwhile, had ordered a general rendezvous on 17 July at Sandiway, a strategically important crossroads on the edge of Delamere Forest and convenient rallying point for supporters from all parts of Cheshire. Word was put out that King Richard himself would join them there, and large numbers made their way to the rendezvous in the expectation of seeing the deposed monarch. When Richard failed to materialize there was evidently some dismay, with many people attempting to return home. Some of those later captured by the royalist forces would claim they had been forcibly pressed into the rebel ranks.

Hotspur attempted to raise enthusiasm by issuing a proclamation, in which he told of his regret for the part he had played in placing Henry on the throne. The king had broken many promises sworn on oath, and had murdered King Richard. Therefore, Hotspur now intended to overthrow him and replace him with the lawful heir to Richard, Edmund, Earl of March. It is unlikely that many of his supporters were particularly inspired by this, or by the promises of governmental reform that Hotspur made. He admitted irritation that so many of those assembled still proclaimed their loyalty to their 'Good King Richard', though some would later proclaim Hotspur himself as king.

The rebel forces did not remain at Sandiway for long. Not only was it necessary to maintain the impetus of the rebellion, but it was also important to give lukewarm recruits no opportunity to desert. Hotspur probably began his march south into Shropshire next day.

The rebel objective was Shrewsbury. Here was the only substantial royalist force in the Marches, with Prince Henry himself. If the prince could be neutralized, or abandoned the town, both it and the munitions stored there would fall into rebel hands, and such a success would in all probability bring in recruits from the Mortimer estates to the south, as well as putting the rebels into closer contact with Glyn Dwr.

Hotspur was undoubtedly encouraged by knowledge of the planned defection of his uncle, Thomas Percy, Earl of Worcester. The exact timing and circumstances of this remain unclear. With so many of his troops recruited in Cheshire, Prince Henry could be far from certain of their loyalty, and Worcester took full advantage of this. At some point, most probably as Hotspur – marching via Broxton, Whitchurch and Wem – approached Shrewsbury, Worcester defected to join his nephew, bringing with him the invaluable reinforcement of 800 of the archers from the prince's force at Shrewsbury. If he had made any attempt to secure the town or the prince, as may have been his original intention, he failed, and around 1,200 men remained loyal to Prince Henry, and with the townspeople, prepared to defend Shrewsbury.

The rebels apparently approached the town from the north late on 19 July and some fighting took place, either that day or early on the 20th, during which some of the suburbs were burnt. But though Prince Henry remained defiant, he was outnumbered and doubtless anxiously awaiting the arrival of his father, the king.

King Henry was at Lichfield on 19 July, mustering his reinforcements. His troops must all have been mounted, for he covered the 32 miles to the vicinity of Shrewsbury by late on the 20th.

Shrewsbury was situated in a naturally strong defensive position, surrounded on three sides by a loop of the River Severn, its only landward entrance being the neck of land at the northern end of the town. The king appears to have sent a detachment of his army to reinforce Prince Henry, while his main force remained to the east of the town, eventually crossing the Severn at Uffington and spending the night around Haughmond Abbey, to the north-east of Shrewsbury.

Hotspur had been wrong-footed by Henry's move, and late on the 20th pulled his army back for the night to the village of Berwick, about 4 miles north-west of Shrewsbury. His intentions are debatable. He may have been considering crossing the Severn at nearby Shelton Ford, with the idea of continuing southwards to join either Mortimer or Glyn Dwr. Alternatively, he may have been planning to withdraw north towards Chester, following the road through Wem. But, given the likely effects of retreat on the morale of his army, Hotspur may always have intended to fight next day.

Approach to Battle
Thwarted and disconcerted by the unexpected arrival of the king in the vicinity of Shrewsbury, Hotspur and his commanders must have spent the night of Saturday 21 July anxiously debating their next move.

War for the Throne

The withdrawal to Berwick on the previous evening may have been an attempt to obtain word of Glyn Dwr, although it is difficult to believe the rebels entertained any hope of his arriving in time to assist them. The village was also close to the ford over the River Severn at Shelton, but a retreat into Wales never seems to have been seriously considered.

Hotspur must have known that, with the exception of his former Cheshire Guard archers and his own small household force, the morale and commitment of the remainder of the rank and file was suspect.

By dawn it seems that the rebels had decided to retreat north up the Whitchurch or Wem road. They would at least be moving towards the reinforcements the Earl of Northumberland was supposedly mustering, although the prospects for overall success were not good.

However, Hotspur's scouts must soon have reported that the main body of the king's army had crossed the Severn that night, and camped around Haughmond Abbey – on the flank of any rebel attempt to retire northwards. Such a retreat was likely to result in the piecemeal destruction and disintegration of the rebel army.

The only feasible option seemed to be to find a good defensive position on which to stand and fight, hoping that the greater experience of many of Hotspur's men would offset the numerical superiority of the enemy.

There is some debate regarding the actual site where the battle took place. It is usually agreed that the rebels withdrew northwards through the village of Harlescott. Approximately 1 mile to the north-east of the village, the rebels would have seen a distinctive ridge running east from the Whitchurch road to the hamlet of Allbright Hussey. In the circumstances, a stand on this defensively advantageous ground seemed to offer the desperate rebels their best chance of success.

Contemporary accounts – as so often is the case – do not identify the site of the battle with precision. John Waurin, whose account of the battle is, at least in part, imaginary, says only that: 'the Lords Percy chose the best and most advantageous position possible, which was near Shrewsbury'. Adam of Usk, who probably had more local information, commented that the battle took place 'in the field of Berwick, where the king afterwards ordered a hospice for the souls of those who there fell two miles from Shrewsbury'.

Campaign Chronicle

As the college of St Mary Magdalen, popularly known as Battlefield Church, was built so that prayers could be offered up for the souls of those killed in the battle, and the charter of its foundation in 1406 states that it was built on the site of the battle, this might seem to fix the location of the fighting with some accuracy. But some uncertainties remain. It is commonly stated that the foundations of the church rest on the mass grave of those killed in the battle. Quite apart from the unsuitability of such a site for the foundations of a massive building, recent archaeological surveys have found no evidence of such a grave, although bones have been found in large numbers nearby. It may well be, as some sources infer, that fighting eventually extended over a fairly wide area. This may explain the variety of field names associated with the battle. Berwick Field, Bull Field and Hussey Field are all names mentioned by contemporary and more modern writers in this context. Stephen Maxwell, a modern historian of the battle, places it further west than most other writers, suggesting that the area to the north of the present church, traditionally cited as the approximate area of fighting, was wooded or heathland in 1403. He suggests that various allusions, notably to the rebels' knotting together of pea plants, as an obstacle to the enemy, indicate that the bulk of the fighting took place on cultivated ground. Extant field names, which seem to post-date the battle, do little to resolve the issue. But the contemporary *Dieulacres Chronicle*, compiled at a Staffordshire monastery by a writer with demonstrable local knowledge, makes it clear that the rebels drew up on Harlescott Old Field, to the north of Shrewsbury and, effectively, on the traditional site of the battle. However, the use by contemporaries of other names can be explained by an encounter that eventually concluded in scattered engagements across a wide area.

A minor caveat to this is that, traditionally, a spot 1 mile to the west of the church is claimed to be the location where Hotspur was killed. Assuming he fought in the centre of his own army, this might appear too far west from the Whitchurch road for the traditional site to be correct. But we do not know quite how far the fighting may have shifted in its later stages.

What might have been helpful is a reference made by the well-known scientist Charles Darwin, who lived in Shrewsbury in the

Battlefield Church

In 1406 King Henry ordered the construction of a church and college dedicated to St Mary Magdalen, to be constructed on 2 acres provided by Richard Husse, on what is generally accepted to be the site of the fighting. The new establishment was placed under the charge of the rector of Allbright Hussey, who was to be master of the college, which was to have five chaplains. The building work was mostly completed by 1409, with the college buildings situated to the south of the present graveyard, and marked now by the remains of their fish ponds. It seems that the area was originally surrounded by a bank and ditch, possibly intended to surround the burial area.

According to tradition, the church was built on top of the largest of the mass graves and there were reports of a large number of bones being uncovered on the north side of the church during nineteenth-century construction work. A mass grave directly beneath the foundations of the church seems unlikely, although a few of the dead may be buried there. Archaeological surveys have found no trace of such a grave in the churchyard, so the location of the mass grave, assuming it to be in the vicinity, remains unresolved.

1820s. He referred to a large number of arrowheads being unearthed in a field to the north of Shrewsbury when it was being ploughed. Unfortunately, no detailed location is given, but it is not inconsistent with being the traditional battlefield site.

It is therefore reasonable to assume that the Percys deployed their forces along part of the ridge extending from the modern Shrewsbury–Whitchurch road to just east of Allbright Hussey. The extent of the position depends in part on the strength of Hotspur's army and on this the sources are not consistent. Waurin, and the author of the *Dieulacres Chronicle*, both credit the king with the wildly inflated total of 60,000 men – more than were present on one side in any English medieval battle. They give Hotspur a mere 7,000. Both estimates, one almost certainly derived from the other, are clearly incorrect. Henri Quarti (*The Annales*) gives King Henry a more likely 10,000 'excellent men', though the chronicler, John Capgrave – probably having confused his source – gives Hotspur the same number.

Neither total seems entirely credible. Given that Richard II saw the figure of 2,500 archers as being a realistic muster from Cheshire in case of emergency, it is unlikely that Hotspur would have levied as many as 7,000 men from a county divided in its loyalties. He was, however, joined by an unknown number of men from North East Wales and Shropshire, as well as his uncle's men from Shrewsbury, so perhaps a total of 5,000 may not be far off.

Similarly, the royal army is unlikely to have mustered anything like 14,000 men. It appears that King Henry had around 2,500 men with him when he learnt of the Percy rebellion. To these should be added those who remained loyal to Prince Henry in Shrewsbury, and such levies as joined the king on his line of march. A grand total of 10,000 seems likely to have been his maximum strength.

Details of the deployment of the opposing armies are also incomplete. There is an ongoing debate among historians regarding the precise formations in which archers were deployed in the medieval battle line, with some evidence being interpreted to suggest that they were formed into 'wedges' jutting out from the flanks and at intervals along the frontage of an army. This may have been the case at Shrewsbury. However, it is equally probable – and supported by the evidence of contemporary illustrations – that archers formed a continuous chequerboard formation along the front of an army, withdrawing behind the men-at-arms just before physical contact was made with an advancing enemy. Other evidence, such as the knotting together of pea plants, suggests that this was indeed the formation adopted by Hotspur's archers, and the royalist forces may be assumed to have conformed. A contemporary account describes the royalist formation:

When the king found himself in the country he made his dispositions of vanguard, main body, and rearguard, of whom he delivered command to those whom he thought proper and worthy to undertake it. He in person led the main body, the Duke of York, his uncle, being with him, and the young Duke of Gloucester, the Earl of Arundel, the Earl of Rutland, and many other great lords. In the vanguard were the Earl of Warwick, the Earl of Exeter, the Earl of Somerset, the Lord de Ros, and many other great lords, and in the rearguard were the young Duke of Surrey and many wise and distinguished knights. And when they were all assembled they numbered fully twenty-six thousand archers and three thousand men-at-arms.

The vanguard is described in some accounts as being led by the Earl of Stafford, although he is also said to have been with the king in the main battle. This, on balance seems more likely, with Warwick or Exeter commanding the royalist right, and Prince Henry leading the left once he and his troops from Shrewsbury arrived.

On the rebel side we have fewer details. It may be that Hotspur's men also formed three bodies, despite their inferiority in numbers. Hotspur and Worcester almost certainly led two of them. Douglas was with Hotspur, so one of the Cheshire leaders may have commanded the left wing.

The Battle of Shrewsbury

By the time that the armies were deployed, it was approaching midday. As was often the case in civil conflict, a last-ditch attempt was made to broker a peaceful solution when Thomas Prestbury, the Abbot of Shrewsbury, accompanied by a royal clerk, was despatched by the king to negotiate with Hotspur. It is unlikely that Henry had any real expectation, or indeed desire, that the talks would bear fruit, but by giving Hotspur this final opportunity he was declaring himself absolved of any responsibility for the bloodletting to come.

There are differing accounts of what followed. Some versions suggest the king invited Hotspur to a personal meeting, but that the latter declined, sending his uncle, the Earl of Worcester, instead. There is no certainty that this meeting actually took place, still less that it followed the course sometimes claimed. What is clear is that talks continued for several hours.

The rebel manifesto was presented to the king, according to John Hardynge carried by Hotspur's esquires, Thomas Knayton and Roger Savey. In the manifesto – probably drafted by Worcester – the rebel leadership made a sweeping condemnation of Henry, accusing him of

The Price of Battle

In recent years considerable light has been thrown on the nature of medieval combat by the discovery of a mass grave of men killed at the Battle of Towton in 1461. The findings also give a vivid picture of the effects on those who took part in the savage fighting at Shrewsbury.

The victims of Towton spanned a wide age range. Eleven of them were between the ages of 26 and 35; the same number between 16 and 25; eight between 36 and 45, with two others of uncertain age. Bearing in mind that Towton involved the raising of extremely large armies on both sides, it may be that older men were not generally levied, and this is likely to have been even more the case at Shrewsbury.

The most common injuries found at Towton were multiple head wounds and evidence of facial mutilation, though only injuries involving skeletal damage are now identifiable. The evidence suggests that sharp 'force' wounds, inflicted by weapons such as poleaxe blades, swords and daggers, are by a ratio of 86 per cent to 14 per cent much more frequent than is evidence of 'blunt' force injury caused by weapons such as hammer staffs, maces, sword pommels or war hammers.

The most numerous wounds were those inflicted on the forearm, consistent with attempts by the victim to parry or fend off an attacker's blows. Wounds to hip and buttock indicate attacks being concentrated, in the case at least of lightly armoured foot soldiers on a weakly protected area, while evidence of torso injury is uncommon, which may indicate that the body was sufficiently protected – even by a quilted 'jack' – to prevent more than flesh wounds in this area.

There were many examples of head injuries, in some cases multiple injuries. Of the dead, twenty-seven had suffered, at some time or other in their lives, between one and thirteen head wounds. Of these, around 36 per cent of the injuries had been inflicted to the front of the head and 32 per cent suffered at the back. The majority of these injuries were to the left side of the head or body, indicating right-handed attackers.

War for the Throne

Very few obvious arrow injuries were identified, possibly because of the nature of the circumstances in which these men were killed, or because any arrow injuries were flesh wounds.

The evidence suggests that the most common tactic in mêlées was for two or more men to bring an adversary to the ground by disabling his legs, and then to kill him with blows to the head.

breaking his oath not to depose Richard, then murdering him. As well as ruling without the consent of lords and commons, and imposing illegal taxes, he had usurped the throne without regard to the claims of Edmund Mortimer, Earl of March, and had declined to allow the ransom of Sir Edmund Mortimer. The wording was not likely to placate Henry, declaring that:

> when thou didest enter England thou madest an oath to us upon the Holy Gospels, boldly touched and kissed by thee at Doncaster, that thou wouldest never claim the crown, kingdom or state royal, but thine own proper inheritance and the inheritance of thy wife in England, and that Richard our sovereign lord the king and thine, should reign during his term of life, governed by the good council of the lords spiritual and temporal [...] WHERE-FORE THOU ART FORESWORN AND FALSE
>
> that where thou sworest upon the same Gospels in the same place and time to us that thou wouldest not suffer any monies to be levied of the clergy, nor fifteenths on the people, nor any other tallies and taxes to be levied on the realm of England on behalf of the realm during thy life, but by consideration of the three estates of the realm, except for great need in causes of importance [...] WHEREFORE THOU ART PERJURED AND FALSE
>
> that thou hast caused the same our Sovereign Lord and thine, King Richard, traitorously within the Castle of Pomfret, without the consent or judgement of the Lords of the realm, by the space of fifteen days and so many nights (which is horrible among Christian people to be heard) with hunger thirst and cold to perish, to be murderd [sic]. WHEREFORE THOU ART PERJURED AND FALSE

that thou at that time, when our Sovereign Lord and thine, King Richard, was horribly murdered as above said, thou by extorted power, didst usurp and take the kingdom of England, and the name and the honour of the kingdom of France, unjustly and wrongfully, contrary to thine oath, from Edmund Mortimer, Earl of March and of Ulster, then next direct heir of England and of France immediately by due course of inheritance after the decease of the aforesaid Richard. WHEREFORE THOU ART PERJURED AND FALSE

that thou fraudulently and contrary to the law of England and thy council, have written through almost every shire in England to choose such knights for to hold a Parliament as shall be for thy pleasure and purpose, so that in thy Parliaments no justice should be ministered against thy mind, in these our complaints now moved.

Also we do allege, say and intend to prove, that when Edmund Mortimer, Earl of March and Ulster was taken prisoner by Owen Glendor [*sic*] in a pitched and foughten field, and cast into prison and laid with iron fetters, for thy matter and cause, whom falsely thou hast proclaimed willingly to yield himself prisoner to the said Owen Glendor, and neither wouldst deliver him thyself, nor yet suffer us, his kinsmen, to ransom and deliver him, yet notwithstanding we have not only concluded and agreed with the said Owen for his ransom at our proper charges and expenses, but also for a peace between thee and the said Owen. Yeah hast thou then not only published and declared us traitors, but also craftily and deceitfully imagined purposed and conspired the utter destruction and confusion of our persons. For the which cause we defy thee, thy supporters and accomplices as common traitors and destroyers of the realm, and the invaders, oppressors and confounders of the very true and right heirs of the crown of England. Which thing we intend with our hands to prove this day, Almighty God helping us.

He [the king] frequently sent envoys, the Abbots of Shrewsbury and Haughmond and others, asking Henry [Percy] to cease from his purpose and whatever just aims he had would gladly have fulfilled. Indeed the gentle king, following the advice of the wise

War for the Throne

men 'the greater a man you are, humble yourself the more in all things', and of scripture, which says 'He who has shed men's blood will have his own bloodshed.' When Henry refused to yield, the king sent peacefully through Thomas Percy, Earl of Worcester, to find out from Henry the reason for the battle and why they had come against him. He replied immediately to the king that the cause was the unjust seizure of the crown, which by the law of inheritance should go to the son of the Earl of March. Thereupon the king proposed to depart without slaughter and to go to Parliament, notwithstanding the fact that he had been elected by them and the lords. The evidence that Henry Percy did not agree with him was that on the day of the coronation he did not come to the feast because it was certainly against his wishes that the coronation took place, since Duke Henry swore to the other two Henrys [Percy] on the relics of Bridlington that he would never aim for the crown. And then he said that if anyone more worthy of the crown were to be found he would willingly yield to him. He said openly that the Duchy of Lancaster was enough for him. They seemed not to agree with this at all, but were disposed to restore the crown to themselves or to fight for it. The king, notwithstanding his impudent reply, endeavouring at this juncture as so often to avoid men's bloodshed, aimed to fight a duel with Henry so that more men should not die on their account. When this was clearly rejected and they had persevered with their earlier purpose the king said: 'I confess that your wicked plan has been divulged which, as long as I live, will never happen. Your purpose is to give your approval to the bastard sons of the Earl of March and the traitor Edmund Mortimer and thus to crown as King Henry Percy or his son by reason of his wife's right to inheritance.' And as they discussed peace, which was in no way agreed, the day drew down to the hour of vespers.

It is doubtful if, after such a sweeping and comprehensive condemnation, that any grounds were left for negotiation. For there were no concessions the king could afford to grant without compromising his entire position.

Campaign Chronicle

Some writers, however, placed blame for the breakdown of talks on Worcester, suggesting that Hotspur had favoured an attempt to reach a peaceful solution and that Henry had been prepared to soften his own demands, but that Worcester had returned to his nephew and deliberately misrepresented what the king said. It does seem unlikely that Worcester and the king actually met face-to-face. Capgrave's version of the exchange between Worcester and the king ran:

Worcester: We brought the one against King Richard, and now thou rulest worse than did he. Thou spoilest yearly the realm with taxes and tallages, thou paist no man, thou holdest no house, thou art not the heir of the realm ...

Henry: I take tallages for needs of the realm, and I am chosen king to common assent of the realm, wherfor I counsel thee to put thee in thy grace.

Worcester: I trust not in thy grace.

Henry: Now I pray God that thou must answer for all the blood that here shall be shed this day and not I.

There were suspicions that the rebels were deliberately dragging out talks until it would be too late to fight that day. The edicts of the Church forbade the shedding of blood on a Sunday, and Hotspur may have hoped that either his father or Glyn Dwr would arrive by Monday. It was said that the Earl of Dunbar strongly opposed the granting of any truce, and advised the king to give the signal for the enemy refused to consent to what was reasonable. 'The signal was needless, so eager were both sides for the fight.' Whatever the truth of the matter, the time for talking was at an end. The decision would now rest with the sword.

Hotspur, outnumbered as he was, had no intention of leaving his advantageous defensive position in order to attack the enemy, until his archers had taken a heavy toll of the royalists and disorganized them. In the event, the king's men were apparently quick to advance. By now it was probably early evening and the king was doubtless anxious to force a decision that day, in case Hotspur was reinforced either by his father or Glyn Dwr.

War for the Throne

Some accounts suggest that it was the royalist left wing, commanded by Prince Henry, which was first to advance, but in reality the move was probably made simultaneously by the king's whole army. That said, the divisions may have advanced slightly in echelon, with Stafford's division on the right engaging first.

Fighting evidently began with an exchange of archery. Although outnumbered, Hotspur's Cheshire archers had the advantages of higher ground and greater experience, and their storm of arrows soon began to tell. The royalist archers not only had to shoot uphill, but they were also probably hindered and thrown into some confusion by the entwined pea tendrils through which they had to pick their way. These would have been growing up stakes around 4 or 5 feet high, and would have been a much more formidable obstacle than sometimes realized. They may also have been unsighted by the rays of the setting sun in their eyes.

The royalist advance seems to have quickly ground to a halt, as, for several minutes, the king's men endured a hail of arrows. The chronicler, Thomas Walsingham, suggests that the rebels were first to begin the barrage:

> Therefore the archers of Henry Percy began the fight and the place for the arrows was not on the ground [...] for men fell on the king's side as fast as leaves fall in autumn after a hoar frost. Nor did the king's archers fail to do their work, but sent a shower of sharp points towards their adversaries.

The arrow storm is unlikely to have continued for more than a few minutes – perhaps five at the outside. It has been suggested that Hotspur's men may have had a greater quantity of reserve arrows available than did their opponents, but there is no hard evidence to support this theory. It is clear, however, that with their advantage of the higher ground – and perhaps because their opponents already were thrown into some confusion by the pea tendrils – the Cheshire archers gained the upper hand. It is possible that the wind direction caused the barrage to drift slightly eastward, so that the royalist vanguard on the right suffered more heavily than either the centre or left. A good deal of the barrage's impact was upon royalist morale.

Campaign Chronicle

Few, if any, of the men on either side had ever been on the receiving end of an arrow storm, but the effect on Henry's less experienced soldiers was devastating.

Prince Henry appears to have made the error common among less experienced soldiers of opening his visor in order to obtain a clearer view. It was probably in the first stage of the battle that he was hit in the face by an arrow that pierced his left cheek just below the eye, and remained embedded in the bone. Contemporary chroniclers suggest that he remained in action and continued to lead his men, but this is difficult to believe. At the very least he must have been severely incapacitated. In fact, considering the prince's youth and relative inexperience, it is likely that he had with him some more experienced commander as his military mentor, who would have continued to direct his command. In any event, the prince's division, which included a number of veteran professional soldiers who had served with him in Wales, remained in the field and capable of playing a decisive role.

Less fortunate was the royalist right wing, possibly commanded by the young Earl of Stafford. These troops were mainly militia, who had never previously experienced the hail of arrows, which now fell upon them. It may be – although contemporary accounts are contradictory – that it was at this stage of the battle that Stafford fell. At any rate this division of around 3,000 men broke and fled, some of them routing through the royalist baggage train from which they took horses to aid their flight.

Stafford, possibly with some of his household troops, may have joined the king in the main battle, which so far stood firm, although its advance had been brought to a halt, and indeed it may have fallen back a short distance out of effective arrow range.

The initiative now lay with Hotspur. He has been accused of rashness in quitting his strong defensive position, just as Richard III would be blamed in a similar situation eighty years later at Bosworth. But in reality, remaining on the defensive any longer was not a viable option for the outnumbered rebels, who had probably used most of their stock of arrows. If they stayed passive, then the royalists might be reinforced by further contingents of militia and renew their attack. Hotspur's best hope lay in exploiting the confusion in the enemy ranks by launching his own attack, given some impetus by the sloping ground.

War for the Throne

As so often happened, once the royalist right collapsed – perhaps even before the rebel counter-attack began – a large number of Hotspur's men charged off the field in pursuit, some joining erstwhile enemies in looting the royalist baggage train, carrying off valuables and horses.

Hotspur launched a general attack with both his men-at-arms and his archers, the latter throwing down their bows and attacking with swords or war hammers and mallets. With cries of 'Esperance Percy!' the attackers surged forward, a few pursuing Stafford's fleeing men or looting the royal baggage. But the main weight of the assault fell on King Henry's 'battle' in Bateley field. Although his suggestion that many of the combatants were mounted is untrue, Walsingham captures the nature of the rebel advance:

> Henry Percy, leader of the opposite army, and the Earl of Douglas, than whom no one was ever more spirited, in spite of the rain of arrows and the dense bodies of horsemen, urged their men against the king's person alone, and concentrated all their arms on him.

Still heavily outnumbered, perhaps, given the departure in pursuit of many of Hotspur's men, with the proportionate strength of the opposing forces much as it had been at the start of the battle, these were sound tactics. If King Henry could be speedily cut down, or even if he were forced to flee the field, the royalist army was likely to collapse. But this manoeuvre left Prince Henry's left wing unengaged. It may be that the prince's men were slightly concealed by a dip in the terrain or that Hotspur's frontage was simply too narrow to engage them as well as the king's division. In any event, whoever was now in effective command of the prince's division was quick to seize the opportunity. He swung his men to the right to attack the right flank of Hotspur's army, perhaps overlapping to take some of them in the rear as King Henry's own division recoiled. According to the chronicler, Edward Hall:

> the Prince Henry that day helped much his father, for although he were wounded in the face with an arrow, yet he never ceased either to fight where the battle was most strongest, or to corage [*sic*] his men when their hearts were daunted.

Campaign Chronicle

Certainly, the rebel right seems to have been pushed into its centre, and the opposing sides became closely locked together in a fiercely contested mêlée. Those who fell were likely either to be trampled to death or, in the case of fully armoured men, to die of suffocation.

Normally, periods of intense hand-to-hand fighting seem not to have been continuous. Opponents often pulled back for short periods, almost by mutual consent, to take breath and possibly to bring up reserves. However, the probable short duration of the fighting at Shrewsbury – possibly no more than two hours in total – suggests that such was not the case on this occasion. The fighting instead seems to have been particularly fierce and intense, as Hotspur's men pressed their attack. They had little alternative: outnumbered as they were, with royalist reinforcements always likely to arrive, they had little option but to try to capitalize on their initial success and complete the rout of King Henry's army.

Some men on both sides, particularly among the commanders, may have gone into action on horseback, although this made them tempting targets for those archers who still had arrows.

Hotspur will have realized that his best chance of victory lay in killing or capturing King Henry. The king's position was apparently marked by the royal standard, and Hotspur, with thirty of his household troops, launched a fierce attack towards it. He seems to have been supported by Archibald Douglas and his Scottish knights, and the rebels started to break into the ranks of the king's division. If King Henry were captured or killed, the battle would effectively be lost and George Dunbar was quick to see the danger. He persuaded the king to withdraw to a safer position in the rear. This in itself was a risky manoeuvre, for if his troops saw Henry apparently preparing to flee, they might themselves begin to rout.

As it was, Hotspur and his men reached the royal standard, whose bearer, Sir Walter Blount, was cut down and killed, possibly by Douglas. Other reports even suggest that King Henry himself was captured briefly until freed in a counter-attack. There is some suggestion that the Earl of Stafford may have donned a surcoat bearing the royal arms in order to assist in the deception but this conflicts with other reports that Stafford had fallen earlier in the battle. In any case, he was struck down now, and cries of 'the King is dead!' were heard in the rebel

Sword and Bow: 'Combined Arms Tactics'

Traditionally, the great English victories of the Hundred Years' War have been attributed to the famed 'longbowman'. Although there is some truth in this, the English success was actually due to a number of factors, not least the development of a remarkably effective partnership of bowman and man-at-arms.

There has been considerable uncertainty regarding the manner in which archers in particular were deployed, largely as the result of the difficulty in arriving at an exact meaning for the phrase used by the chronicler, Jean Froissart, in describing the deployment of the English archers at Crécy: 'au manier d'un herce'. While it is generally agreed that Froissart is referring to the agricultural implement known as a harrow, this could take several radically differing forms.

In seeking a solution it is instructive to look ahead several decades to the engagements of the Wars of the Roses, when there is clearer contemporary evidence of how archers were deployed. At Towton (1461) it is clear that the opposing archers began the battle deployed five or six deep in staggered formation across the full frontage of the armies and shot their initial barrages from this position. It seems possible that a similar deployment was used at Shrewsbury.

As a battle progressed, and attacking forces drew closer, it seems most likely that the archers pulled back onto either flank, forming 'wings' deployed several ranks deep in 'chequerboard' formation, and projecting slightly forwards. This would leave the way clear for men-at-arms situated in the centre to engage the enemy, while the archers continued to fire into the attackers' flanks, and sometimes launch their own attacks in support of their men-at-arms. The latter were normally formed into three divisions, of varying depth, depending on the numbers available. Usually the best armed and equipped would be in the front ranks, with less well-equipped levies further to the rear.

English 'combined arms' tactics were most effective when the enemy took the offensive, as the Lancastrian forces did at Shrewsbury. After the archers had delivered their barrage (see the textbox: 'Arrowstorm', p. 52) the (hopefully) weakened and disorganized attacking force would close in mêlée with their own men-at-arms.

The hand-to-hand combat that followed was the most bloody phase of the engagement. Ideally, the attackers had been weakened both by the effects of the arrow storm and by obstacles placed in front of the defenders' position. At Shrewsbury these apparently consisted of pea plants plaited together, which probably tripped and slowed the attackers. They had also probably become closely bunched together, making it only possible for their first one or two leading ranks to engage the defenders on a fairly narrow front.

---

ranks. Other accounts claim that a second knight was also dressed in the royal livery, although this seems unlikely, as it would clearly have been seen as dishonourable for the king deliberately to skulk in the rear, according to a pre-arranged plan, while others took his place in disguise.

It seems more likely that the king's possibly brief retirement at Dunbar's suggestion was a spur of the moment decision. Even allowing for the exaggerated nature of claims that the king had so far personally despatched thirty-six of the enemy in hand-to-hand fighting, it is clear that he had been in the thick of the action, and may well have been exhausted and vulnerable to the ferocious onslaught of Hotspur and his bodyguard. It was probably at this stage that someone, possibly Stafford, was allowed to don the royal surcoat and act as 'substitute' under the royal banner, to avoid any loss of morale among neighbouring royalist troops. However, the fall of both the royal banner and of the substitute 'king' was seen by some of the troops and they began to waver, their alarm heightened by triumphant rebel cries of 'Henry Percy King!' The growing disorder among his men caused King Henry and George Dunbar, with their escort, to plunge into the fighting once more. It was now about 8pm and the gathering dusk was heightened by a total eclipse of the moon, which may have been viewed by those on both sides as a bad omen.

The battle seemed finely balanced. Many of King Henry's men, particularly those on his right, had fled, and numerically speaking,

War for the Throne

the opposing sides may now have been roughly equal. But the royalist centre was still holding its ground, while on the left, Prince Henry's division was attacking the rebel flank and beginning to close in on Hotspur's rear. Clearly, if they were to win at all, the rebels had to do so quickly. There was also the danger that Hotspur and his household troops would be cut off from the rest of their army. At this critical moment, Hotspur was killed.

The circumstances of his death remain unclear. Thomas Walsingham noted that 'while he led his men in the fight rashly penetrating the enemy hosts, [Hotspur] was unexpectedly cut down, by whose hand is not known'. A feasible tradition has Hotspur killed by an arrow, which hit him in the face while he had his visor raised, drawing breath or attempting to gain a better view of events. It is arguable whether Hotspur's death made any real difference to the outcome of the battle. His army was clearly losing when Percy fell. Although it is said that shouts of 'Henry Percy dead!' rang out from the royalists, it is unclear how widely Hotspur's death was known as his men began to make off into the darkness to avoid being completely surrounded. It seems unlikely that King Henry's troops were able to mount much in the way of an organized pursuit. The men of both sides were hopelessly intermingled amid the darkness and confusion. Many men, trusting in the anonymity of night, were more concerned to loot the dead and wounded, regardless of party.

Most of Hotspur's men fled up the Whitchurch road, back towards Cheshire. The royalists succeeded in capturing a number, however, including several rebel leaders. Chief among them were Thomas Percy, Earl of Worcester, and Archibald Douglas – the latter reportedly after falling from a rock and injuring his testicles, which suggests that he was taken some distance from the battlefield. Also taken were at least two of the Cheshire leaders, Sir Richard Venables and Sir Richard Vernon.

It was probably not until daylight on 22 July that the grim task of tallying and disposing of the dead, and treating any wounded felt to warrant such, began. It was left to Thomas Percy to identify the body of Hotspur, over which King Henry himself was reported to have shed tears. If such was indeed the case, it seems that his grief was soon mastered.

Initially Hotspur's body was handed over to Thomas Neville, Lord Furnival, for burial at Whitchurch, but no later than Monday, 23 July was brought back to Shrewsbury for more ignominious treatment.

After passing Sunday in little doubt of their fate, the captured rebels next day faced royal justice. Quite how many were executed remains unclear, although the implication is that more were disposed of than those whose names we know. Worcester, Venables and Vernon were given a swift hearing, found guilty of treason, and beheaded the same day in Shrewsbury market place. Worcester's head was despatched to London to be displayed on London Bridge until the end of the year, when it was brought back to be buried with his body in Shrewsbury abbey church. The heads of Vernon and Venables were displayed at Chester.

Hotspur's corpse, rubbed in salt as a preservative, was placed on public display between two millstones in Shrewsbury market place. And then, this local exhibition complete, the body was butchered, the head being sent for public display in York, and the quarters to London, Bristol, Chester and Newcastle.

Just how many men died in those few bloody hours at Shrewsbury will never be known. Some accounts give totals as high as 7,000 or 8,000, but more likely estimates range between 1,600 and 2,291 dead, with perhaps 3,000 wounded, many of whom will have died later. Many of the dead were reportedly buried in a common gravepit 126 feet long and 65 feet wide, over which Battlefield Church was supposedly later built. Perhaps not surprisingly, given the initial success of the rebels, there are indications that the royalists lost most heavily. Of those knights known by name to have died in the battle, sixteen were royalists and eight rebels. Another account says twenty-eight royalist knights and eight rebel knights died. However, another version lists 200 Cheshire knights and squires among the dead. Not all of these would have been on the rebel side.

The Price of Rebellion

After retribution had been dealt out to the rebel leaders, and an unknown number of their followers, taken at Shrewsbury, there remained the problem of the many other rebels still at large.

War for the Throne

The Cheshire loyalist, Sir John Stanley, his desire for vengeance whetted by an arrow-wound in his throat that made him speak 'rattlingly', urged the king to 'bren and slee! bren and slee!' ['burn and slay! burn and slay!'] in his treatment of the rebels. King Henry in fact chose to adopt a more moderate course of action.

The king had other immediate concerns, not least the condition of his eldest son, Prince Henry. The head of the arrow that had injured him was still lodged deep in his face, entering it from the left, burying itself in the cheek and reaching the bone behind the prince's nose. For several days after the battle Henry was treated with plant and herb extracts, and sedated, probably with opium, while the royal physician, John Bradmore – possibly with some trepidation – considered his options. His solution was to design a specialized instrument. A key-like screw was produced, which was inserted into the wound and into the socket of the arrowhead, and then gradually retracted and withdrawn, bringing the arrowhead with it. The pain must have been excruciating and Henry will have borne the scar for the rest of his life, although, surprisingly, no contemporary writer appears to have remarked on it.

Arrangements would also have been made for the removal, and if they were lucky, treatment, of the other less illustrious wounded who had survived a night on the battlefield.

The king chose not to heed the advice of Sir John Stanley regarding the men of Cheshire. The reality was that, with the mounting threat from Glyn Dwr to the marches, Henry could not afford to lose the services of the highly experienced Cheshire troops. With the exception of a few ringleaders, who were outlawed, most were received into favour and indeed back into military service. The king's aim was to reconcile the men of Cheshire to his regime and he succeeded to the extent that many would serve Henry V in France, and indeed, half a century later, Cheshire was strongly Lancastrian in sympathy at the start of the Wars of the Roses.

Even though Hotspur and Worcester were dead, and their army scattered, the danger to Henry's regime was not over. The Earl of Northumberland was still at large in the north, and potentially at the head of a powerful army. On 23 July King Henry wrote to Ralph

Campaign Chronicle

Neville, Earl of Westmoreland, ordering him to proceed against Northumberland without delay.

The course of events in the north over the next few days is unclear. Northumberland was probably still in North Yorkshire, raising his tenants. How far this process had gone before he received news of the disaster at Shrewsbury is uncertain. But the news clearly shattered, for the moment, any hope of further resistance to the royalist forces. Westmoreland seems to have moved into North Yorkshire with superior forces and Northumberland decided that it would be futile to engage him.

Together with some of the men he had mustered at Tadcaster, Northumberland headed north to Newcastle. News of the defeat at Shrewsbury had travelled ahead of him and the emboldened towns-people refused to admit the earl's men, allowing only Northumberland himself, with a few attendants, to enter. In response, Northumberland's men seem to have attempted to storm the town but were repulsed. The game was clearly now up for Northumberland and he disbanded his troops and took refuge at his favourite residence, Warkworth Castle.

King Henry was marching northwards and by 4 August had reached Pontefract. From there he sent a message to the Earl of Northumberland, ordering him to answer for his actions on 11 August at York. There is little doubt that Northumberland, if not actually instigating the revolt of his brother and son, had been deeply implicated in it. He could only hope that the slightly ambivalent attitude he had displayed and the king's need for reconciliation in England might save him.

Hotspur's head was already on display above one of the gates of York (probably Micklegate Bar), perhaps that through which Northumberland entered the city. If so, the sight probably deepened the earl's hatred for the king, and his determination one day to seek vengeance for the death of his kin. For the moment, however, the pressing need was to save his own life.

The meeting between erstwhile rebel and monarch was a frosty one. Northumberland denied any part in the rebellion, placing all blame on Hotspur and Worcester. It may be that there was some doubt in the king's mind regarding the earl's guilt, or perhaps that he felt that enough blood had already been spilt. Northumberland had no surviving sons, his grandson was an infant, and Henry may have had

War for the Throne

no desire to make the Nevilles overpowerful in the north. In his letter ordering Northumberland to attend him at York, Henry had already promised the earl that he would be allowed to put his case to Parliament. In the meantime, he would be kept in custody at Baignton near Coventry, and his castles were to be handed over to the crown. The latter objective took some time to achieve. The constables of the Northumbrian Percy castles were mainly from the earl's estates in Yorkshire and proved reluctant to surrender their charges.

As early as 26 July, the king appointed his squire, John Coppall, as governor of the great castle at Bamburgh, in place of the Percyite Thomas Knayton, who had probably been killed at Shrewsbury. Possibly because of the death of its governor, Bamburgh passed fairly quickly into royal control. King Henry, however, could afford neither the time nor the loss of royal dignity involved in remaining in person to secure all of the Percy garrisons. Instead, the task was delegated to loyalist Northumbrian gentry. However, Warkworth, Alnwick and Berwick-upon-Tweed were still holding out defiantly early in 1404.

It is hard to believe that this resistance was not on the instructions of the Earl of Northumberland, anxious to retain some bargaining chips when his own fate was eventually decided.

Parliament met at Westminster on 14 January 1404 and three weeks later Northumberland, who had been brought to Windsor, appeared before it. The king had already been given clear indications that many in Parliament opposed the burden of taxation that Henry was demanding to finance his war in Wales and against the French, and there were hints of some agreement with those who suggested that his right to the throne was by no means incontestable, even going so far as to suggest that Northumberland should be pardoned without further ado.

The king could not openly agree to this, and insisted the earl must petition Parliament for pardon. This was, of course, mere face-saving. The Lords promptly found Northumberland guilty of trespass, but not of treason, and sentenced him to a fine. The king, equally promptly, remitted the fine, and granted Northumberland a full pardon and restoration of his estates. The king may have believed that the earl, after his narrow escape, would no longer present a threat. He would soon learn otherwise.

*

Campaign Chronicle

Although Hotspur had gone down to defeat and death at Shrewsbury, and the Percy threat was for the moment quelled, in Wales Glyn Dwr continued to prosper. The unrest in North East Wales, partly kindled by Hotspur, continued after his death. In early August Welsh rebels based there raided into Shropshire and laid siege to the castles of Flint, Rhuddlan and Hawarden. These were fairly easy to supply by sea or land from nearby Chester, but other English garrisons in North Wales were more seriously threatened.

The temporary incapacity of the wounded Prince Henry meant he was replaced in Wales by a commission headed by the Earl of Arundel, Thomas, Lord Berkeley, Edward Charlton of Powys and Lord Audley. This joint leadership was not likely to be effective, and with the king preoccupied throughout August in dealing with the embers of the Percy revolt, Glyn Dwr took full advantage of the situation. His men raided deep into South Wales, as far as the shores of the Bristol Channel, carrying off livestock and other booty. Glyn Dwr himself was reported to be in North Wales, preparing to raid across the Dee estuary into Wirral.

Once again, beleaguered royal officials, with the men of Hereford-shire on the verge of making terms with the Welsh, pleaded with the king to come to their assistance. Orders were given for levies to muster at Worcester on 10 September. But in the meantime, the English position continued to worsen. On 3 September, the same day that Henry reached Worcester, the Archdeacon of Hereford, Richard Kingeston, wrote desperately to the king that only his personal presence would save the county from devastation. Over 400 Welshmen were at large in Herefordshire, plundering and driving off cattle into the hills of South Wales. Kingeston had sent out virtually all of his men to oppose them, so that, 'in faith, I have naught left with me but two men'. He urged that, at least, a respected commander such as the Earl of Somerset be sent to support him with 100 men-at-arms and 600 archers.

The king, meanwhile, remained at Worcester, crippled by lack of money, sending out orders to the Marcher lords to replenish and reinforce a large number of castles in South Wales and its borders.

Henry was able to extract a small amount of money from un-willing bishops and magnates who were with him at Worcester, and

War for the Throne

on 11 September reached Hereford, where he called out the neighbouring levies, and ordered that supplies be collected at Bristol and taken to the castles of South Wales – or at least to those of them that could be reached by sea.

By 19 September Henry had begun his own advance across the Golden Valley of Herefordshire, his objective being to relieve the castle at Carmarthen. As usual, he met with no opposition, as the enemy melted away into the hills. The king reached Carmarthen on 24 September and gave orders for the repair of its defences, leaving behind a force under the Earl of Somerset with supplies and pay for a month. Henry himself was back at Hereford on 3 October, ordering a new muster of levies for a renewed expedition into Wales, which never apparently happened. By now Glyn Dwr's men were once again active in South Wales and the Herefordshire border.

By the middle of November, Henry was back in London. Although he was greeted by enthusiastic, though possibly staged, demonstrations of loyalty from the citizens, his only notable success of the summer – though admittedly a vital one – had been the crushing of the Percy rebellion. In Wales, the troops left at Carmarthen were in a state of mutiny, saying they would not remain beyond the agreed month 'for anything in the world'. Their commanders warned that unless the situation was taken in hand, 'the King is in great peril and on the high road to ruin'. The Duke of York was sent to take over command.

But this did nothing to mend the English position in Wales as a whole. In Anglesey, Beaumaris Castle was in trouble, though supplied to some extent by ships from Chester, while Cardiff was reliant upon supplies brought by sea across the Bristol Channel. Lampeter Castle, surrounded and with its garrison facing starvation, was in grave danger. Aberystwyth Castle, though again sometimes reprovisioned by sea, was under acute threat. Kidwelly Castle had been attacked and the Welsh insurgents in the area had been reinforced by men from French and Breton ships operating off the coast.

By the end of the year, the Duke of York had somewhat reluctantly assumed command in South Wales, with the authority to grant pardons, and partly financed by a fine of 3,000 marks levied on the citizens of Chester for their part in Hotspur's rebellion. The Duke's commission was for a year, and as well as the garrisons of South

Wales, he was to have a mobile force of 250 men-at-arms and 780 archers.

But Glyn Dwr was dominant throughout much of Wales. In November, the war widened when French ships, led by Jean d'Espagne, joined in an attack on Caernarvon. The castle was under the command of a Cheshire man, William of Tranmere, with a dwindling force of soldiers and townsmen. His garrison included three men-at-arms, two of whom succumbed during the winter. Both were members of prominent Welsh families, one connected with the Royal House of Gwynedd, illustrating the fact that the war in Wales was also, in part, a civil conflict. Some families had members on opposing sides and were open to reprisals from both sides in consequence.

Welsh High Tide

The year 1404 saw Glyn Dwr at the height of his power. Although in March, in an attempt to draw a line under the Percy rebellion of the previous summer, the king granted a general pardon to all involved in acts of rebellion in the Welsh Marches and the north during the previous year, rumours of the imminent return of King Richard continued. And Henry remained crippled by lack of money, and facing threats of French attacks by sea.

Although the assault on Caernarvon in November had failed, the French and the Welsh insurgents had not abandoned their efforts there. The garrison in the summer of 1403 had totalled twenty men-at-arms and eighty archers, but during the course of the year this had dwindled to twenty-eight, including townsmen. For their renewed attack, the Welsh and French built siege engines – a very rare feature in Glyn Dwr's operations – sows (covered mobile siege towers) and long scaling-ladders. They also evacuated livestock from Anglesey, which was vulnerable to attack from the sea.

On 16 January the siege began, the acting governor of Caernarvon, Robert Parry, sending a woman to Chester in a plea for help.

Caernarvon was not the only garrison under threat. Two more links in Edward I's 'stone ring' around Snowdonia, Harlech and Aberystwyth, were also in danger. During the autumn of 1403 the garrison of Harlech had arrested their constable, William Hunt, on suspicion he was about to surrender the castle to the Welsh. However, the strength of the garrison dwindled, some dying as the result of sickness, others deserting, while a few were killed attempting to run the Welsh gauntlet and reach Chester. Early in January an attempt to reach a truce with the Welsh failed and three more of the original garrison of ten men-at-arms and thirty archers were captured. By now the defenders consisted of five Englishmen and a few townsmen.

The relief of the threatened coastal castles was supposed to be the responsibility of Lord Berkeley, Admiral for the South and West, but although he had been provided with £2,344 to pay for supplies and men, he proved, perhaps because of winter weather, unable to achieve much.

All of the coastal fortresses from Caernarvon to Cardigan remained under close blockade by the Welsh. Harlech, in particular, was doomed and Glyn Dwr made a deal with the remaining garrison that they would surrender if not relieved by a stipulated date.

During the spring, with Prince Henry not yet returned to his command, Welsh raiders – reportedly with French reinforcements – devastated a third of Shropshire up to the gates of Shrewsbury, and there were wild rumours that Glyn Dwr was marching on Northampton.

At the end of March – Parliament having, for the moment, supplied the king with some funds – John Stevens of Bristol was ordered to take five ships laden with salt, corn, vinegar and wine to supply the coastal castles.

Once again, Caernarvon proved too strong for its attackers but at some point in the late spring, Harlech fell to Glyn Dwr.

And the Welsh tide of success was sweeping through South Wales. Despite orders to the Earl of Devon to reinforce it, the town and castle of Cardiff fell to Glyn Dwr, and the town was plundered and burnt. Caerphilly, Usk, Caerleon and Newport Castles fell, or were abandoned by their garrisons. Most of the countryside was in rebel hands, and the body of one of the Welsh members of Caernarvon's garrison had to be taken by sea for burial at his home in the Lleyn Peninsula, as the town was completely isolated by land.

Possibly inflated estimates credited Glyn Dwr with a potential army of 30,000 men, although he would never have been able to supply or maintain such a large force. To many churchmen, of whatever sympathies, Owain was seen as 'the rod of God's anger'.

Campaign Chronicle

Probably by the start of summer, although in unknown circumstances, Aberystwyth town and castle also fell to the Welsh. Glyn Dwr now effectively controlled most of Wales outside the walls of its remaining English-held towns and castles. It was clearly time for him to move forward from being a successful leader of guerrillas towards trying to establish a more coherent administration in the areas under his control. Indeed, to maintain credibility and impetus, Owain had no real alternative.

By the spring of 1404, Glyn Dwr had formally assumed the title 'Prince of Wales'. This not only represented an end of any possibility of reconciliation with the English government but also made a statement of his intent to establish a Welsh state on an equal footing with European counterparts.

A further testament to the growing credibility of Owain's cause came with the defection to him of a number of prominent churchmen, who were often experienced administrators. Among them were John Trefor, Bishop of St Asaph, Lewis Byford, Bishop of Bangor, and the brilliant (and illegitimate) Gruffydd Yonge, who became Owain's chancellor and probable candidate for archbishop of a new, independent Welsh Church.

These men provided Glyn Dwr with the substance as well as the trappings of government. Their first task was to cement the current informal alliance with the French into a more concrete agreement. Yonge and Owain's brother-in-law, John Hanmer, were despatched to Paris to thrash out the details. With the war party at the French court in the ascendancy, they met with a favourable reception, and in July a formal treaty of friendship was signed between Owain and King Charles VI of France. As well as an undertaking that neither party would seek a separate peace with England, the treaty also promised French military assistance to the Welsh. An expeditionary force of 800 men-at-arms and 300 crossbowmen under the Count of La Marche was assembled in Brittany, although bad weather would prevent it from sailing that year.

Owain was by now informing his supporters that 'you may know that their [the English] time is ending, and victory is turning to us according to God's ordering from the first, which none can doubt'. In furtherance of his claims, a Welsh Parliament was summoned that summer to meet at Machynlleth, with four representatives from each commote – the historical Welsh administrative unit, corresponding to the English 'hundred'.

Throughout the summer, the tide of Welsh success continued to swell. Herefordshire and Shropshire reeled under the impact of Welsh raids, with parts of western Herefordshire, at least, probably effectively under rebel control. Once again, King Henry lacked the money to finance any effective response. He made no effort to mount his annual *chevauchée* into Wales. Though by the autumn Prince Henry was apparently back in command on the Welsh border, the situation had deteriorated to such an extent that the King's Council was forced to acquiesce in the men of Shropshire paying the Welsh for a three-month truce.

With most of Wales effectively in Glyn Dwr's hands, King Henry's enemies nearer to home were also showing signs of renewed activity. For the Earl of Northumberland, following the death of his son and the desecration of his body, his original grievances with the Lancastrian regime had now assumed the character of the traditional northern 'blood feud'. By the end of 1404 he was merely awaiting an opportunity to strike. Summons to the earl to attend King Henry were ignored on varying pretexts, until the threat of an accusation of high treason eventually brought Northumberland to a meeting with the king at Pontefract, around Midsummer's Day. He also handed over for trial and subsequent execution one Richard Searle, one of the impostors who had passed himself off as King Richard. Northumberland also agreed to hand over his remaining northern castles, in return for property of equal value elsewhere.

The Glyn Dwr Revolt: Turning Point

The fact remained that while Glyn Dwr could claim to have laid the foundations of a Welsh state modelled on European lines, his hold on it was fragile and incomplete so long as the majority of its fortresses remained in enemy hands. The only way Owain's dream could be turned into reality was by the capture of these garrisons. And this could only be achieved by switching from guerrilla tactics to more orthodox campaigning; but it would prove enormously difficult – given the topography of Wales, its overall poverty and the nature of Welsh warfare – to muster a conventional army or formulate a strategic plan. Throughout its course, the revolt would be characterized by local flare-ups and risings, often apparently spontaneous, under local leadership, and not having any obvious connection with an overall plan. These might well be difficult for the hard-pressed English authorities to counter, but they also did little to establish permanent rebel control of Welsh territory and could, on occasion, assume the characteristics of pure banditry.

High in Welsh priorities were raids to carry off cattle and supplies into the rebel heartlands of mountainous North and West Wales, which themselves lacked sufficient resources to maintain Glyn Dwr's men. Equally important – and again contributing little towards an effective overall strategy – was the kidnapping and holding to ransom of English and pro-English gentry and officials. In many cases ordinary inhabitants were also seized for the same purpose, which might bring in some funds, but also carried with it the potential of alienating local communities; so, too, did the deliberate destruction of buildings of economic importance such as mills and barns.

If one of the motivations behind Welsh operations was to obtain supplies and arms, or the money with which to purchase them, efforts to reduce the network of castles upon which control of the countryside ultimately depended proved much less successful. Except on rare occasions (when they had French support, for example) the Welsh lacked equipment for regular siege warfare. The majority of castles that fell into their hands seem to have done so as a result of treachery, starvation or isolation rather than orthodox siege warfare. With the exception of Aberystwyth and Harlech, deep in the Glyn Dwr heartland, few of the castles that did fall remained in Welsh hands for long, while the majority were never taken at all.

The castle would be the key to the eventual recovery of English control in Wales. The initial large-scale *chevauchées* by the king and some of his commanders, while possibly having more success than they are sometimes credited with, lacked the methodical sustained persistence that had characterized the operations of King Edward I during his Welsh wars of 1277 and 1282–1283. They certainly dampened rebel activity temporarily, but failed to extinguish it.

War for the Throne

During the earlier part of Henry's reign shortage of money, the reluctance of commanders and men to serve in Wales and other distractions – notably the threats from the Scots, the Percys and the French – prevented the development of any coherent strategy in Wales, beyond one of desperately holding onto the castles.

Wales would never be a theatre of war that offered tempting prospects of glory and rich booty to the English military aristocracy. It would be left to men of more humble origins, the constables of the castles and the captains of the troops quartered in them, to wage the prolonged war of attrition that would gradually turn the tide. They – and some regional leaders such as Richard, Lord Grey of Codnor and Gilbert Talbot of Goodrich Castle – would bear the brunt of a decade or more of grinding, unspectacular, small-scale campaigning.

Between 1403 and 1405 the English authorities could do little beyond trying to contain the rebellion, and, with little success, to curb Welsh raids into the English border counties. Large garrisons were placed in Marcher strongholds such as Oswestry, Montgomery, Welshpool and Brecon. Possibly because it was in part protected by the River Dee, Cheshire does not seem to have suffered as badly from the effects of Welsh raiders as did Shropshire and Herefordshire. Throughout these early years English counter-attacks found it difficult to engage an illusive foe, although Welsh lands and property were devastated in turn, probably at times with as little enquiry into the allegiance of the owners as the Welsh displayed in their turn. It was a ruthless war, in which little quarter was given by either side.

It was only possession of the network of castles that, during these early years, prevented the total collapse of English rule throughout Wales. While it would be too much to assume that such a collapse would have gained the Welsh their aim of independence, it would certainly have made the process of English reconquest prolonged and difficult. It has been estimated that in 1400 between 100 and 120 castles in Wales and the Marches were in reasonable defensive condition. Many others, after long decades of peace, were more or less neglected or had become little more than poorly fortified residences. On the outbreak of the rebellion, many urgent repairs began. Initially the castles provided places of refuge for English settlers and Welsh loyalists. But they became bases from which patrols could be mounted and, later, would act as starting points for systematic reoccupation of the surrounding countryside. Consequently, it was vital for Glyn Dwr to break up the network of garrisons. And with the aim of forming a state to rank alongside its European counterparts, he had no option but to move towards more conventional warfare in an effort to achieve this objective. It may well be that he relied upon the arrival of French military aid in order to make this possible. But 1405 dawned with no substantial aid having yet arrived. It may have been this that forced the Welsh into a high-risk strategy of their own.

Early in the year reports began to grow that there would be a major Welsh spring offensive headed by the redoubtable Rhys Gethin in Herefordshire. As usual, lack of funds hindered effective counter-measures – even the garrisons of the royal fortresses of North Wales remained seriously depleted.

On the morning of 11 March a large Welsh force – probably overestimated in English reports as being 8,000 strong – attacked the small town and castle of Grosmont in the Monnow valley. The Welsh burned the town, possibly preparatory to an attack on the castle, but were easily surprised by a small English mounted force under Gilbert Talbot and Sir John Grendor. Although they were probably not greatly outnumbered as English sources claimed, the troops clearly took the enemy by surprise, probably in a sudden sally from the castle, and completely routed them. Between 800 and 1,000 Welsh were supposedly killed with no prisoners being taken, apart from one 'great chieftain' who was badly hurt. It may have been Rhys Gethin himself, as he does not seem to appear in contemporary accounts thereafter.

It was Glyn Dwr's first serious reverse and some of the Welsh on the borders of Herefordshire now made terms. But the struggle for Wales, and indeed for the English throne, was far from over. In February, King Henry had suffered another unwelcome reminder of how 'uneasily' rested his crown.

If the Percys were temporarily quiet, Sir Edmund Mortimer remained at large in Wales and his nephew, Edmund, Earl of March, was, for many, the rightful claimant to the English throne. Edmund and his brother Richard were in honourable captivity at Windsor when, in February 1405 – following on from a plot to murder the king, allegedly involving the Duke of York – Lady Despencer spirited the

War for the Throne

boys out of captivity and headed for the Welsh border. They were recaptured near Cheltenham but the episode illustrated that opposition to the new regime remained.

Meanwhile, in the north of England, after Parliament had declined to authorize the Earl of Northumberland being granted lands of equivalent value to his surrendered castles, Berwick and Jedburgh had been nominally restored to him, but had actually been left under the control of royal constables. In February 1405 – though not yet known in England – came clear evidence that Northumberland was again plotting treason. It is generally agreed by historians that it was during that month, in the house of the Archdeacon of Bangor at Aberdaron, that a Tripartite Indenture was sealed by representatives of Glyn Dwr, Sir Edmund Mortimer and the Earl of Northumberland. The three men agreed a formal alliance and a three-way division of the kingdom. The Mortimers – presumably with the younger Edmund having the title of king – were to have Southern England, the Earl of Northumberland the North and deep into the Midlands, while Glyn Dwr would rule a Welsh principality extending to the Severn and the sources of the Trent and Mersey and thence to the sea. It may be doubted how long such a division of the realm would have survived without conflict breaking out among the victorious parties, or indeed whether it could ever have come into effect, but it was further evidence of the dangers the Lancastrian regime still faced.

In an interesting indication of the average size of contemporary armies, in June 1405 Prince Henry was to command a force in North Wales totalling 3,000 archers. In South Wales the king would lead 144 men-at-arms and 720 archers. In May the Welsh suffered another setback in a serious defeat at Pwyl Nelyn near Usk, when it was claimed that the rebels lost 1,500 men, among them Owain's brother Tudur, at first mistaken for Glyn Dwr himself. Owain's son Gruffydd was captured. Around the same time – perhaps captured at sea on their way back from France – John Hanmer, Owain's brother-in-law, Gruffydd Yonge and Owain's secretary were also taken. These reverses were significant, though not yet decisive, setbacks for Glyn Dwr, and there seemed a possibility that a successful summer campaign by the king and Prince Henry might finally gain the upper hand. But Glyn Dwr would be reprieved by events elsewhere.

Campaign Chronicle

The Earl of Northumberland had been biding his time. In January 1405 he excused himself from attending the Royal Council at Westminster on the grounds of age and poor health, once again – perhaps ominously – signing his letter to the king as 'your Matthias'. In March, however, Northumberland did attend a royal council. But soon afterwards he was joined in the north by emissaries from Glyn Dwr and by Thomas, Lord Bardolph, an East Anglian magnate with close connections by marriage to both the Mortimers and the Percys.

Northumberland's own role in what now followed is unclear. But by the end of April discontent in the north – triggered as much by high taxation as clearly defined pro-Ricardian or Percy sentiment – had flared into rebellion. An attempt to seize Henry's chief supporter in the area, Richard Neville, Earl of Westmoreland, was narrowly thwarted.

One of the leaders of the plot was Richard Scrope, Archbishop of York.

Hitherto, Scrope had been viewed as a politician rather than a devout churchman, and had actively assisted in the legal process of deposing King Richard. However, Scrope's family was closely connected by marriage with the Percys and in 1403 Hotspur and Worcester claimed to have his support, although Scrope had apparently extricated himself from the allegation. But in the early summer of 1405, accompanied by the earl marshal, he openly showed his hand.

It is highly likely that he was involved in drawing up the unsigned declaration posted on the great door of York Minster, restating the demands of the Percys in 1403, complaining of illegal taxation, calling for the restoration of the 'rightful' monarch (presumably the Earl of March) and a settlement with Glyn Dwr. Although Northumberland himself ostensibly remained aloof, many of his adherents and tenants took up arms, and Scrope gathered about 8,000 armed men in York, many of them village priests and their parishioners. A force of similar size was mustering on the Percy estates in North Yorkshire, but was intercepted by loyalists at Topcliffe (while awaiting the arrival of Northumberland himself) and easily dispersed. Another royalist force, under the Earl of Westmoreland, took up position on Shipton Moor, about 6 miles north-west of York, and a stand-off with the rebels in the city followed.

War for the Throne

On 29 May, after three days of stalemate, the opposing forces faced each other. In an echo of events at Shrewsbury two years earlier, Westmoreland offered to meet the rebel leaders to discuss their grievances, apparently hinting that he sympathized with them. Against the advice of his fellow rebels, Scrope himself went to meet Westmoreland and, in circumstances that remain unclear, he and the other principal rebel leaders were arrested, having first, under the impression that agreement had been reached, persuaded their men to disperse.

A furious King Henry, marching north in person to quell the rebellion, refused a meeting with Scrope and the other principal rebel leader, the earl marshal. Despite the remonstrances of the archbishop of Canterbury, both men were taken before a hastily summoned commission, which summarily condemned them to death. Both were executed under the walls of York and Scrope's decapitated body buried in York Minster.

It may be that Henry had acted in haste and anger, and he certainly seems to have been severely affected psychologically. The same night that Scrope was executed, the king rode through rain and storm to lodge for the night near York. During the night, Henry awoke screaming: 'Traitors! You have thrown fire over me!' Although suggestions that the king was stricken by leprosy seem unlikely, he clearly was afflicted with some kind of skin problem – possibly a nervous reaction to what had happened. It may have signalled the beginning of what would prove to be a gradual decline in his health.

Initially, Henry seems to have hoped for reconciliation with the Earl of Northumberland, possibly because he was uncertain of the degree of his involvement with the uprising. But Northumberland had withdrawn to the Berwick area, where he was believed to be mustering men. On 11 June the earl's property, along with that of Lord Bardolph was declared to be forfeit, and the king's troops marched north in strength to crush the last embers of revolt. On 19 June the king was at Durham, two days later he reached Newcastle. From here Henry prepared to move north to deal with the earl.

Langley Castle, near Hayden Bridge, surrendered without a fight, as did Prudhoe Castle, 11 miles from Newcastle. By 27 June the king was within a few miles of Northumberland's principal residence of

Campaign Chronicle

Warkworth Castle. It and nearby Alnwick Castle were summoned to surrender. The garrison of Alnwick responded that the king should capture Berwick first. The captain of Warkworth refused outright to surrender. Henry brought up cannon and other siege equipment. After several shots had been fired, the garrison yielded and were allowed to march out, suggesting that their resistance had been a face-saving device rather than serious defiance.

Northumberland himself, with 300 men, was still outside Berwick, but was now admitted by the mayor, who later claimed to be ignorant of the rebellion. The earl offered to hand the town over to the Scots, in return for their support, but this came to nothing. On receiving a guarantee of personal safety, however, he and Bardolph fled across the border into Scotland to join his heir, Hotspur's 2-year-old son.

Berwick Castle refused to surrender to King Henry, who brought up cannon. The defences of the town and castle were in poor repair. A 40-yard breach was opened on the south side of the castle and a continued bombardment soon caused the garrison to seek terms. A number of rebels in the town and castle were executed. By 14 July Alnwick had surrendered and the revolt in the North seemed completely crushed. But events in the North had given Glyn Dwr a valuable breathing-space.

He had, with increasing desperation, been awaiting the promised French assistance. On 15 July the levies of Gloucester, Bristol and Somerset had been ordered to South Wales. Soon afterwards news arrived of a French landing at Milford Haven and the king ordered all the levies of the border counties to rendezvous at Hereford. On 22 August the king reached Worcester.

Glyn Dwr reportedly had begun the summer in a pessimistic mood. A second Parliament had been summoned to meet at Harlech, and according to some possibly over-sanguine English intelligence reports, was considering making terms if French assistance did not arrive.

The French expedition, which finally set sail in July, was largely a private enterprise scheme headed by the Lord of Hugerville and Jean de Reux, Marshal of France. A force of 800 men-at-arms, 600 cross-bowmen, and 1,200 light infantry was mustered and embarked on a fleet of 120 ships. Despite storms in the Channel, which cost them nearly all of their horses due to lack of fresh water, the French arrived

War for the Throne

Bombards

Although lighter pieces of artillery were occasionally employed in battle, apparently to little effect, the heavier guns used in siege warfare were most commonly of the type known as 'bombards'. The term was first employed around 1380 to denote a heavy siege piece, which normally fired stone balls. The best-known example in Britain was the Scottish bombard known as 'Mons Meg', which could fire shot weighing 396 pounds.

Although bombards could be effective, their use during the early part of the fifteenth century in England and Wales was not notably successful. Although none of the great Edwardian castles succumbed to bombardment, they provided the future Henry V with valuable experience which he utilized later in his conquest of Normandy, when a combination of guns and catapult-type siege engines – notably the trebuchet – proved relatively effective. Even then, however, many French garrisons resisted until starvation brought about their surrender.

off Milford Haven early in August. They rendezvoused with Glyn Dwr and up to 10,000 men. Even if the actual Welsh total was less, it is clear that Glyn Dwr had made a supreme, perhaps all or nothing, effort.

The Franco-Welsh force advanced on the Flemish settlement at Haverfordwest, taking and burning the town, although the castle held out. The allied expedition then moved against Tenby, laying siege to the castle. But an English fleet entered the harbour and burned fifteen French ships. The Franco-Welsh army moved on to Carmarthen, whose garrison of twenty-eight men-at-arms and 100 archers surrendered on terms. The town was burnt and its defences slighted, before Glyn Dwr and his allies marched on eastwards through Glamorgan, burning and plundering as they went, crossing Herefordshire and coming within 10 miles of Worcester. The king led his forces out from Worcester to meet them. The invaders took up position on Woodbury Hill, probably around an ancient hill fort on its summit. A stand-off followed, with the royal forces on high ground divided from Glyn Dwr by a shallow valley. Daily skirmishes and single combat between opposing knights and men-at-arms took place. Around 200 men on both sides were reported to have been killed. Among the French dead were three knights. However, neither army was willing to risk the outcome of a full-scale battle and lack of supplies forced the invaders to retreat into Wales, with Henry too weak, or too cautious, to pursue. Though nobody knew at the time, Glyn Dwr had made his greatest effort and had failed. He would never again pose such a serious threat.

By 10 September the king had received sufficient funds to take the offensive. Much of South East Wales had submitted to the English again, in the delicate balancing act performed by local communities in an effort to preserve themselves from destruction. The king embarked upon what would prove to be his final Welsh expedition in person. He relieved Coity Castle in Glamorgan but then retreated, suffering his customary mauling at the hands of bad weather and Welsh guerrillas. Once again it seemed that a year of campaigning had ended in stalemate.

Glyn Dwr's Decline

At first Glyn Dwr seemed almost as threatening as ever. That winter the men of Pembrokeshire bought a truce with him. But Welsh hopes of further significant assistance from the French were fading. Many French knights, disillusioned by their experience of campaigning in a country where booty and opportunities for glory were limited, returned home before winter. Left behind were 1,200 infantry and 500 crossbowmen under a Picardian commander, Le Beguede de Belay. They apparently spent the winter in comfortable lodgings, and in the spring of 1406 went home before Lent, being badly mauled en route by English ships.

For Glyn Dwr, French support had proved a bitter disappointment. Even his recognition of the French-sponsored Avignon Pope Benedict and plans for a new Welsh Church and two universities were no more than pipe dreams.

The Earl of Northumberland and Lord Bardolph – by no means certain that one of the contending factions in Scotland would not hand them over to the English – headed early in 1406 to Wales. Here they seem to have attempted, without much success, to recruit English malcontents, and by the early summer had left for France.

War for the Throne

On 19 February 1406, Prince Henry was made Lieutenant of all Wales and the Marches, providing unified command of the English forces there. He was promised a mobile force of 100 men-at-arms and 3,000 archers, suggesting that it had been decided that the latter more lightly armed mounted troops were better suited for the kind of warfare experienced in Wales than more heavily armoured men.

The tide had clearly begun to turn. In November, Anglesey submitted to the king, with 2,112 of its men seeking terms. Those who remained recalcitrant were outlawed. Glamorgan and Monmouthshire were also steadily passing back under English control. The English recovery was slow, and not without reverses. But eventually it would prove inexorable. The foundations of recovery were the castles, sea power, supply, and, above all, money.

After the king's expedition of 1405 there would be no more major efforts in Wales. Instead the key to recovery would be the castle. Lack of finance had been the major obstacle to the effectiveness of this strategy in previous years. In 1404 the royal council had calculated that the daily cost of maintaining fourteen castles with garrisons totalling 1,415 men would be the alarming sum of £42 (around £2,000 in present-day terms). But the English also had technological advantages in the 'castle war'. The Welsh were rarely in possession of adequate siege equipment, while the English, when they were able to commence operations to regain the lost castles, could deploy the full panoply of siege engines, cannon and other equipment. Sea power also enabled the English – albeit it with difficulty – to maintain control of other coastal fortresses, although several seem to have fallen briefly into Welsh hands. It was bad weather, and spasmodic French naval presence, that had led to Glyn Dwr's capture of Harlech and Aberystwyth.

In July 1406 English ships based at Chester landed troops in Anglesey to begin the recovery of that fertile part of North Wales, important in feeding the rebels. It was probably English sea power that also thwarted any Welsh counter-attack across the Menai Straits. It is noticeable, however, just how long it had taken the English authorities to adopt the methodical process of conquest and occupation that had been a feature of the successful operations of Edward I a century earlier. Coupled with offensive measures was a substantial campaign to starve the Welsh of supplies and munitions. The rebellion, given the limited Welsh resources, could never be entirely self-sustaining. Although perhaps lacking other results, King Henry's *chevauchées* at least pointed out the relevance of a 'scorched earth' strategy. Although it was never possible completely to stifle illegal trade with the Welsh by English merchants, the restrictions that were imposed forced much of Welsh strategy to revolve around raiding across the border in order to obtain supplies. In the end, a shortage of essential foodstuffs, coupled with the ferociously hard winter of 1407–1408 did much to hasten the collapse of the rebellion.

Glyn Dwr was aided by the somewhat chaotic system of administration represented by the Marcher lordships, which hindered any coherent English strategy, and still more by the financial and political challenges facing King Henry until at least 1406. Historically, Wales had always prospered when the government of its mighty English neighbour was weak, and this was never more the case than during much of the Glyn Dwr rebellion. An already hard-pressed exchequer, faced by threats from Scotland and France, was even more straitened by the loss of its Welsh revenues, which could, in theory, amount to £12,000–14,000 out of an annual total of £75,000–90,000. The annual maintenance costs of just five castles in North Wales came to £5,561 (over £233,000 in present-day terms).

Lack of English funds did much to prolong the war. During its early years, commanders from Prince Henry down repeatedly complained of a shortage of money. It was not until the financial situation began to improve that a more coherent military strategy became apparent, and the tide of the rebellion began to ease. At the same time English forces began to go over to the offensive, rather than merely attempting to contain the rebels. An attempted Welsh offensive in the spring of 1406 seems to have met with at least two serious reverses, one of them, in the Mortimer territory of Powys, reportedly involving Northumberland and Bardolph. These setbacks certainly hastened the submission of South East and parts of North East Wales by the end of the year. Much of Ceredigion and probably the Twyi valley also submitted.

And so, by the start of 1407, Glyn Dwr was being steadily pushed back. Northern Powys submitted by July and the Lordship of Denbigh

War for the Throne

in North Wales in September. Tiny detached Maelor Saesnig surrendered in May. The only parts of Wales under Glyn Dwr's firm control were Caernarvonshire, Merionethshire and northern Ceredigion. Even here English power was resurgent. In May, Prince Henry was appointed to serve in Wales for six months with 600 men-at-arms and 1,800 archers. In North Wales Gilbert Talbot with 100 men-at-arms and 400 archers was sent to collect fines in Caernarvonshire and Merioneth.

But the main English effort of the summer was intended to be the recapture of Aberystwyth Castle. This was meant to be a great symbolic English triumph and Prince Henry, the somewhat unreliable Duke of York and the Earl of Warwick, were among the many notables who gathered for the kill. Siege guns and engines were brought up and supplies ferried in by sea. Eight guns – probably those earlier employed in the north against the Percy castles – were to be taken from Pontefract to Bristol by land and thence transported by sea to Aberystwyth. Provisions and supplies of all kinds were also prepared. Timber (for siege engines and ladders) was to be cut in the Forest of Dean, then transported to the siege in two barges.

The original intention had been for the king to take personal charge of operations, but possibly because of concerns about simmering unrest in the north, Prince Henry was left in command in Wales. The Admiral, Thomas, Lord Berkeley, took day-to-day command of operations at Aberystwyth, and the king's 4½-ton gun, 'Messenger' was sent from Nottingham to intensify the bombardment, with additional powder and ingredients for its manufacture.

But one gun burst during firing, while the slow progress of the siege seems to have sapped confidence of a quick and decisive conclusion among the English nobility. The Welsh garrison, under Rhys Ddu, was running short of provisions by late September and on the 12th they invited twelve of the English leaders into the castle for discussions. It was agreed that Aberystwyth and its garrison would be surrendered if not relieved by the week ending 1 November, and hostages were exchanged in an armistice that would be observed in the interim. The garrison was to be pardoned once the surrender took place. Leaving behind 120 men-at-arms and 360 archers in garrison at Ystrad Florida Abbey, Prince Henry returned to Hereford. The king, feeling that the surrender of Aberystwyth would signal the effective end of the rebellion, planned to be present in person.

But, as so often, his hopes were dashed. Before the agreed surrender date, Glyn Dwr managed to enter the castle in secret and repudiated the agreement, condemning those who had made it as traitors. The English troops were deserting, and once again rumours were circulating regarding the loyalty of the Duke of York, although Prince Henry declared that it was only the duke's efforts that had saved the expedition from disaster.

Northumberland's Last Throw

The Welsh cause would receive a final, ultimately fatal blow at the hands of the notoriously hard winter of 1407–1408. The same harsh weather saw the end of Henry Percy, Earl of Northumberland.

Northumberland and Lord Bardolph had failed to obtain any help from the increasingly sceptical French, and had met with no more success in Flanders. Their prospects were grim. Glyn Dwr was plainly in trouble. The Scots were divided among themselves, and the Regent, the Duke of Albany, was seeking a truce with England. Nobody had any confidence in Northumberland's claims of potential support in England.

However, Northumberland and Bardolph still convinced themselves there were large numbers of Englishmen ready to take up arms against King Henry. They were in touch with some apparent malcontents, such as Sir Thomas Rokeby, Sheriff of York, who appeared sympathetic, and there were hopes of allies in Cumberland and the Midlands. Some of the men garrisoning the former Percy strongholds such as Alnwick were also thought likely to rally to the banner of the Blue Lion.

Northumberland and Bardolph had made their way to Scotland, where the Duke of Albany tried without success to talk them out of a new attempt in England. But other Scottish lords urged them on, and Northumberland may have recruited a few troops north of the border.

Winter was, of course, the worst time to launch a military campaign, and the winter of 1407–1408 – long remembered as 'the big winter' – was the worst in living memory. The major rivers of Europe were frozen completely and there was heavy snow. In England the snow lasted from December to March with livestock and thousands of birds dying and people starving.

In late January, in the midst of this bitter weather, Northumberland and Bardolph crossed the Tweed into England with a few Scottish mercenaries and a handful of Yorkshire retainers. Late in the month, Northumberland raised the standard of rebellion at Thirsk, calling upon all those opposed to the Lancastrian regime to join him. The response was not large. A number of clergy and monks from the North rallied to his cause and brought some of their tenants and parishioners with them. But the gentry, and especially the leading magnates, held aloof from what they clearly felt to be a hopeless venture. Most of Northumberland's followers were tradesmen and peasants from the Thirsk and Topcliffe areas of the old Percy estates. The sheriff, Sir Thomas Rokeby – whether because he had been acting as an agent provocateur all along or because he felt Northumberland to be doomed – did indeed call out the militia, but ordered it to march *against* the rebels, not with them. He took position guarding the crossing of the River Nidd at Gimbaldsbridge, near Knaresborough. Northumberland could not force a crossing and instead moved east, crossing the river further down. He reached Wetherby late on Saturday, 18 February, and next day, passing through Tadcaster, took up a defensive position on high ground on Bramham Moor.

The strength of the opposing armies is unknown, though both were fairly small, and details of the action that followed are also scanty.

Fighting is said to have begun around 2pm on 19 February, when Rokeby and his men arrived. The royalist forces are thought to have attacked uphill against the rebel position, and a disorganized mêlée spread across the area around Camp Hill, Headley Hill and Oglethorpe Hill. It appears that Northumberland's force was quickly routed and Bardolph mortally wounded. The Earl of Northumberland, now aged 66, traditionally died in a rearguard action. He was supposedly killed in a hollow between Oglethorpe Hill and Old Wood 250 metres north of Toulston Lane. It is unclear whether he died fighting or was summarily executed.

Bardolph died the same night. The grey-haired and bearded head of Northumberland was sent to London on a pike and paraded through the streets before being displayed on London Bridge. His quarters were displayed at Berwick, Lincoln, Newcastle and York. On 2 July 1408, Northumberland's remains were buried alongside Hotspur in York Minster.

The usual executions of lesser rebels and confiscation of their property followed. Among the prisoners was Lewis Byfort, Glyn Dwr's emissary and Bishop of Bangor. Sir Thomas Rokeby was rewarded with the Percy manor of Spofforth.

The Percy threat to the English throne was at an end. Hotspur's infant son would eventually return from exile to become a devoted supporter of the House of Lancaster.

The End of Glyn Dwr

In the summer of 1408, Prince Henry resumed the Siege of Aberystwyth, which fell (probably) in late September. Operations against Harlech – where Glyn Dwr's wife and daughters and Sir Edmund Mortimer were – began around the same time. The besiegers were under the command of Gilbert Lord Talbot and his brother, John, Lord Furnival. In December they had a force of 300 men-at-arms and 600 archers, with gunners, carpenters, smiths and labourers. Despite a number of Welsh raids on English supply lines, the eventual outcome of the siege was not in doubt.

Sir Edmund Mortimer died, or was killed, during the siege, and at the end of February 1409 Harlech surrendered. Mortimer's wife, Catherine, their four children and Glyn Dwr's wife were taken to London, and three of the children died soon afterwards.

The Glyn Dwr rebellion died hard. By the end of 1408 the war in Wales was once again one of guerrilla raids, mainly for supplies and captives to ransom, conducted from the mountainous heartlands of North and West Wales. The rebels were not a serious threat to Henry's regime, or even to his control of large parts of Wales. Rather than being crushed decisively in battle, the rebellion gradually faded away across most of Wales, with a steady stream of submissions to English authorities not inclined to be unduly vindictive, except in the case of rebel ringleaders.

But as late as the autumn of 1409 local Marcher lords in North East Wales were still making individual truces with rebels or bandits (the

The Fate of Owain Glyn Dwr

Although the recapture by English forces of Harlech Castle in 1409 symbolized the final ruin of Glyn Dwr's ambitions, the embers of revolt continued to glow for many years afterwards. Glyn Dwr himself was still launching the occasional raid in the Marches as late as 1412, and some of the wilder parts of Wales remained 'no-go areas' to English officials, without a strong military escort, for some time longer.

Indeed, Wales was of concern to the English government, which had real fears of renewed rebellion until around 1421, when Glyn Dwr's son, Maredudd, at last submitted. Even then, there remained some Welsh irreconcilables. Welshmen had fought on both sides at Agincourt, and it was not unusual for Welsh soldiers to be among the prisoners captured in garrisons during Henry V's later campaigns in France. They were usually hanged.

Owain Glyn Dwr himself disappears from history in the autumn of 1415, still rejecting all offers of pardon from the newly-crowned Henry V. His end is as mysterious today as it was to contemporaries. One possibility is that he died as a fugitive, hiding in woods and caves. Another tradition has him living out his final months in seclusion at the home of his daughter at Kentchurch, on the Herefordshire border.

Despite various theories, Glyn Dwr's final resting-place remains unknown. The mystery of his end played a part in Owain's rise over the centuries to become the greatest national hero of Wales.

difference between the two was growing ever more indistinct). It would be some years before English officials could travel through parts of Wales without the protection of substantial military escorts. No rents could be collected from Northern Ceredigion as late as 1413. The final stronghold of the rebels was remote Merioneth. Here die-hards lurked and even in 1417, the area – with the rebels now led by Owain's son, Maredudd – was seen as a possible source of further trouble.

In 1410 Glyn Dwr had made his last big raid on the Shropshire border. Rhys Ddu and Owain's son-in-law, Phillip Scudamore, were captured and both were hanged, drawn and quartered.

Campaign Chronicle

In 1413, on his accession to the throne, Prince Henry, now Henry V, offered pardons to Owain Glyn Dwr and his son. The offer was rejected or ignored. Later offers were made to Maredudd ab Owain only – suggesting that by the end of 1415 Owain Glyn Dwr was thought to be dead.

Maredudd continued, at least in theory, to maintain resistance for several years longer, plotting with Sir John Oldcastle, the rebel Lollard leader, and still seeking help from Scotland and France. Many Welshmen fought on for years in French service against the armies of Henry V, and at Agincourt there were Welshmen on both sides. But it was not until 8 April 1421, when Maredudd accepted pardon, the Welsh rebellion can at last be said to have been over, though lawlessness continued as its legacy for years to come.

The struggle for the English throne seemed to be at an end. But only thirty years later it would be renewed in the bloody conflict known to history as the Wars of the Roses.

Aftermath

———◦•◦(●)◦•◦———

The struggle for the throne, and for the control of Wales, continued for over a decade following Henry Bolingbroke's coup of 1399, his deposition and murder of Richard II and his own assumption of the throne as King Henry IV. The unrest, plotting and open rebellions were the result of the weakness of the new regime, and to some extent the well-grounded doubts of both Henry and many of his new subjects as to the king's right to the throne. As a result, Henry was confronted by an array of opponents both at home and abroad. It was not until 1409 – ten years after his accession – that, worn out with years of tension and crisis, a sickly Henry could feel reasonably secure.

Of his opponents, the most immediately dangerous to Henry were always those within England itself. While the Scots might raid and plunder the northern counties, Glyn Dwr's 'Children' dominate much of Wales and make forays into the Marches, neither of these foes were likely to overthrow the new regime. However, the supporters of former King Richard – some of whom still believed their master to be alive or had transferred their allegiance to his favoured heir, Edmund Earl of March – were a more serious threat, with their constant plotting and assassination schemes.

When, by early 1403, the king's opponents grew to include the powerful Percy family – kingmakers in 1399 and masters of much of the north – the crisis became acute, with control of England hanging in the balance. While the earlier battles of the struggle (notably Bryn Glas and Homildon Hill) were of major importance in the long-running border war with Scotland, and the struggle for Wales, the campaign of July 1403, which climaxed at Shrewsbury, would decide the fate of the throne of England.

Most historians agree that the Shrewsbury campaign was a close-run thing for King Henry. He was probably fortunate in that, by his decision to march to the assistance of the Percys in their Scottish campaign, he had unwittingly triggered Hotspur into acting unilaterally, or at least prematurely, before his father or Glyn Dwr could assist. Hotspur was forced to stake everything on the support he could muster in Cheshire. This left him in a position of numerical, though not qualitative, disadvantage. Though the details are obscure, it seems that the rebels suffered a further blow when Thomas Percy, Earl of Worcester, failed to take Shrewsbury and capture Prince Henry. Though he brought a considerable number of the prince's troops over to the rebel cause, the prince and the remainder were able to hold Shrewsbury until King Henry marched to their assistance.

So far as the strategy of the campaign was concerned, the royalists hardly put a foot wrong. The king's initial inclination to pull back towards London and enlist additional forces was correctly opposed by George Dunbar, Scottish Earl of March, who prevailed on Henry to move rapidly against Hotspur with the aim of bringing him to battle before he could be reinforced. Once Hotspur failed either to take Shrewsbury or to be reinforced by Glyn Dwr or the Earl of Northumberland, his rebellion – barring good fortune – was doomed. With the royalist army close on his heels, he had no option but to stand and fight.

The Battle of Shrewsbury horrified contemporaries, not only because it was the biggest action of its kind fought on English soil for half a century, but because it was an internecine conflict, which set Englishman against Englishman, and indeed Cheshireman against Cheshireman. And the scale of slaughter was such that chroniclers recoiled with disbelief. Although we cannot tell how many fatalities resulted from it, the spectacle of the 'arrowstorm' employed for the first time on a large scale by opposing armies, seared the imaginations of those who witnessed or heard about it. So far as the conduct of the battle itself is concerned, Hotspur is sometimes condemned for his 'rashness' in leaving his ridge-top advantage in an attack on the royalist army – yet he had little alternative. Once their supply of

Aftermath

arrows was exhausted, the rebels were likely to be overwhelmed by sheer weight of numbers. Hotspur's only real hope of snatching victory lay in the tactics he actually adopted: disrupting the opposing army as much as possible by means of the 'arrowstorm', then launching an attack aimed at exploiting and widening the disarray, and if possible, killing or capturing King Henry himself. Judged by these criteria, Hotspur had a fair degree of success. His archers routed a significant part of the royalist army, but Hotspur's hopes of following this up by disposing of King Henry were thwarted by the royalist use of at least one decoy wearing the royal heraldic device, and by the king's distinctly unchivalrous – but highly realistic – decision to heed the advice of Dunbar and quit the worst of the mêlée until the crisis was over. Only the action by whoever by then was in command of Prince Henry's wing of the army in taking the rebels in flank and rear, which might have happened anyway given the royalists' superiority in numbers, displays evidence of any particularly outstanding leadership on the royalist side.

It is often said that Shrewsbury played a major role in the military education of the future King Henry V. But pitched battles were a minor part of fifteenth-century military operations. Henry would fight only one other – Agincourt – in the course of his life. It was the long campaign in Wales, with its problems of supply, communications and siege warfare that taught Henry and his fellow commanders the tactics they would later employ with success in France.

Counter-factual history is always a risky subject. But it is tempting to consider the likely results if Hotspur had won at Shrewsbury. Despite the cries of 'Henry Percy King!' set up by some of his men during the battle, there was no realistic possibility that the Percys would have been accepted by the bulk of the English magnates as a replacement for the Lancastrian royal house. The succession would have gone to Edmund, Earl of March, still a minor, and the terms of the later Tripartite Indenture would probably have been put into effect, at least in de facto form. This was, in itself, a recipe for further conflict, and disagreement between Percys, Mortimers and Welshmen was inevitable. Prolonged conflict along the lines of the future Wars of the Roses would almost certainly have followed, with an uncertain outcome.

War for the Throne

The real victors would probably have been the French, for without Henry V and England divided and at war with itself, there would have been no Agincourt or English conquest of Normandy.

The Battlefields Today

Bryn Glas and Homildon Hill are both largely given over to agricultural purposes. A good view of the eastern slopes of Bryn Glas Hill, where the bulk of the fighting took place, can be had from the churchyard of St Mary's Church, Pilleth. A number of those killed in the battle are buried there, and others in a mass grave marked by the row of Wellingtonia trees.

At Homildon Hill, the high ground occupied by the Scots is clearly visible from the road that lies along the probable line of the English advance.

At Shrewsbury, the 600th anniversary of the battle in 1403 was marked by the development of the Battlefield Park. There is a useful observation mound, from where the battlefield may be viewed, near the Visitors' Car Park on Battlefield Way, off the A41. Clearly-signposted trails, with information panels at intervals, allow the reasonably active visitor to explore the most likely battlefield area. Battlefield Church is also worth a visit, as is the exhibition area and refreshment facilities at nearby Battlefield Farm.

Orders of Battle

—◦◀(◦)▶◦—

Given the loose organization of medieval armies, orders of battle in the modern sense are not possible to compile. It can be assumed, however, that each of the leaders listed here for each battle led a substantial part of their respective armies.

Pilleth

Welsh
Owain Glyn Dwr?
Rhys Gethin

English
Sir Edmund Mortimer
Sir Walter Devereux
Sir Thomas Clanvowe
Sir Robert Whitney
Sir Kinnard de la Bere

Homildon Hill

English
Henry, Earl of Northumberland
George Dunbar, Earl of March
Sir Henry Percy (Hotspur)

War for the Throne

Scottish
Archibald, Earl of Douglas
Earl of Moray
Earl of Fife
Earl of Orkney
Earl of Angus
Sir John Swinton

Shrewsbury

Royalist
King Henry IV (main battle)
George Dunbar, Earl of March (main battle)
Prince Henry (rear battle)
Duke of York (vaward)
Earl of Stafford (possibly vaward)

Rebel
Sir Henry Percy (Hotspur)
Thomas Percy, Earl of Worcester
Archibald, Earl of Douglas
Sir Richard Vernon
Sir Richard Venables

Glossary

Aventail — mail protection for the head, somewhat like a balaclava.

Commote — a Welsh administrative division, roughly equivalent to the English hundred.

Jack — protective jacket worn by soldiers usually either of padded material or covered by thin metal plates.

Lance — a term that could be used to describe either a single mounted soldier or a group of three: man-at-arms, archer and attendant.

Man-at-arms — a soldier, sometimes, but not necessarily, a knight, armed with sword and a variety of pole-type weapons. Usually armoured.

Schiltron — a massed formation of Scottish spearmen.

Uchelwyr — Welsh gentry, in some cases descended from the former Welsh ruling families.

Bibliography

Bean, J.M.W., *Henry IV and the Percies* in *History* 44 (1959), pp. 212–27.

Bennett, Michael, *Richard II and the Revolution of 1399*, Sutton Publishing, Stroud, 1999.

Boardman, Andrew W., *Hotspur: Henry Percy, Medieval Rebel*, Sutton Publishing, Stroud, 2003.

Brough, G.J., *Glyn Dwr's War*, St Athans, 2002.

Burne, Alfred H., *Battlefields of England*, Eyre and Spottiswoode, London, 1950.

Capgrave, John, *Chronicle of England*, London, 1857.

Clark, James G. and Presst, David, *The Chronica Maiora of Thomas Walsingham, 1376–1422*, Philmore Woodbridge, 2003.

Cooke, David, *Battlefield Yorkshire*, Pen and Sword, Barnsley, 2006.

Curry, Anne, *Agincourt: a New History*, Tempus, Stroud, 2005.

Davies, R.R., *The Revolt of Owain Glyn Dwr*, Oxford University Press, Oxford, 1995.

Dodd, Gwylim and Briggs, Douglas, *Henry IV: the Establishment of the Regime*, Woodbridge, 2003.

Ellis, Sir H., *Hardynge's Chronicle*, London, 1812.

Fletcher, W.G.D., *Battlefield Church and the Battle of Shrewsbury*, Shrewsbury, 1903.

Florato, V., Boylston, A. and Knusel, C., *Blood Red Rose: the archaeology of a mass grave from the Battle of Towton*, Oxbow Press, Oxford, 2000.

War for the Throne

Gillespie, J.L., *Richard II's Archers of the Crown*, in *Journal of British Studies*, vol. 18, 1978–1979.

——, *Richard II's Cheshire Archers*, in *T.H.C.L.S*, vol. 136, 1994.

Griffiths, Rhidian, *Prince Henry's War: castles, garrisons and supply during the Glyn Rebellion* in *B.B.C.S.* 34, 1987.

Hardy, Robert and Strickland, Matthew, *The Great War Bow*, Sutton Publishing, Stroud, 2005.

Hingeston, F.C. (ed), *Royal and Historical Letters During the Reign of Henry IV*, 2 vols.

Hodges, Geoffrey, *Owain Glyn Dwr and the War of Independence on the Welsh Borders*, Little Logaston, 1995.

Keegan, John, *The Face of Battle*, Cape, London, 1976.

Kirby, J.L., *Henry IV of England*, Constable, London, 1970.

Lloyd, John Edward, *Owen Glendower*, Oxford University Press, Oxford, 1931.

Lomas, Richard, *The Fall of the House of Percy, 1363–1408*, Donald, Edinburgh, 2007.

McNiven, Peter, *The Cheshire Rebellion of 1400*, in *B.J.R.L.*, 52 (1969–1970).

——, *The Men of Cheshire and the Rebellion of 1403*, in *T.L.C.H.S.*, vol. 129, 1975.

——, *The Scottish Policies of the Percies and the Strategy of the Rebellion of 1403*, in *B.J.R.L.* vol. 62 (1979–1980).

Morgan, Phillip, *War and Society in Medieval Cheshire 1277–1403*, Manchester University Press, Manchester, 1987.

Phillips, J.R.S., *When Did Owain Glyn Dwr Die?* in *B.B.C.S.* 24 (1970–1972).

Pollard, Tony and Oliver, Neil, *Two Men in a Trench: Battlefield Archaeology – the Key to Understanding the Past*, BBC, London, 2002.

Prestwich, Michael, *Armies and Warfare in the Middle Ages: the English Experience*, Yale University Press, Yale, 1996.

Priestly, E.J., *The Battle of Shrewsbury, 1403*, Shrewsbury Borough Council, Shrewsbury, 1979.

Skidmore, Ian, *Owain Glyndwr, Prince of Wales*, Gomer Press, Swansea, 1978.

Bibliography

Smith, J.B., *The Last Phase of the Glyndwr Rebellion* in *B.B.C.S.* 22, 1966–1968.

Wade, Richard, *Arrowstorm: the World of the Archer in the Hundred Years War*, Staplehurst, 2007.

Wylie, James Hamilton, *History of England Under Henry IV*, 4 vols, London, 1884–1898.

Websites

www.battlefield1403.com Battlefield 1403, farm, café and exhibition relating to the Battle of Shrewsbury.

www.battlefieldstrust.com description of the battle and battlefield.

www.english-heritage.org.uk the Battlefields Register, description of the battle and battlefield.

Index

Index

Index

War for the Throne